Of Sphere

.

a winner of the **2016 Open Book Contest**
selected by Carla Harryman

# Of Sphere

Karla Kelsey

**Essay Press**
2017

ISBN: 978-0-9969229-2-0

Cover art by Austin Thomas, *Black with Colored Circles*, 2016
monoprinted with Akua Intaglio Ink on proofing paper, 37 x 18
Cover design by Aimee Harrison
Composition by Travis A. Sharp
Text typeset in Fira Sans & Garamond

Essay Press is a non-profit 501(c)(3) organization dedicated to
publishing innovative, explorative, and culturally relevent prose.
www.essaypress.org

Distributed by Small Press Distribution
1341 Seventh Street
Berkeley, California 94710
spdbooks.org

10 9 8 7 6 5 4 3 2

# CONTENTS

INTRODUCTION

"Art is the revelry in the excess of nature, but also a revelry in the excess of the energy in our bodies," remarks philosopher Elizabeth Grosz in an interview in which she discusses her sense of the most elementary materials and conditions for art. Karla Kelsey's *Of Sphere* sets in motion a critical poetics of relation and habitus that draws from such basic, philosophical inquiry. Its variousness, intensities, and decorative expositions align with Grosz's pairing of nature's and the body's excesses.

In an ornamental fashion, Kelsey's essay interleaves a profusion of concepts and descriptions reminiscent of the poetic, psychic elaborations of place and scene in Virginia Woolf's *The Waves*; and, like Woolf's novel, this essay expands the field of its genre. It is also a work of astute observation in which the inside-outside binary that places the feminine in the object position is not only challenged but becomes something other to how we normally understand the binary. One notes for instance the portrayal of interpersonal dynamic through the "I-you," which not only replaces "he-she" grammar but becomes a medium for re-conceptualizing relation. Through her challenge to dug-in patriarchal logics, Kelsey choreographs a contemporary vision that follows in the experimental tradition of earlier modern feminist essays, including Woolf's *Three Guineas*, H.D.'s *Tribute to Freud*, and Hélène Cixous' "The Laugh of the Medusa." Kelsey brings an urgency to this tradition through her attention to the destructive human impact on the earth, ecological crisis, and her vision of another way to inhabit the world.

Through her attention to variety—the multifariousness of the like, the proximate, and the unlike—Kelsey constructively queries the desire for unity. Her interest in unity is one that incorporates the vexing contradictions embedded within the aesthetic objects that we share in common. This provocation, which links the wish for with the critique of unity, is illuminated in Kelsey's choreography of sentences and the relation of sentences to kinesthetic as well as visual fields:

> Take a photograph, terrain in a blur synced with your hand in a blur, invisible things, parts of everything else, determining us.

Here movement and vision blur together as if we were experiencing the abstract traces activated in a photograph, from the initial point of taking the picture through the flows of presences and absences that the captured image evokes. While Kelsey explores such realms of abundance and excess (e.g. "parts of everything") as a continuous, open field of exchange that unifies all aspects of an event, she simultaneously recognizes the determining limits of objects, desire, and events. In a passage of comedic eroticism in "Geosphere V," dream-like concatenations of taffeta and tulle, dog collar and peek-a-boo bra, leather and thong, disperse into the waking-moment bell sounds of small satisfaction and absence:

> In dream the bell continues, the ring it makes upon the hour always attended, held until its fade. I suppose this will have to suffice for the day's release regardless of my desire to rut in the field before you part.

Limit does not have one meaning or value; the comedy of erotic intimacy and imperfect connection will be entwined with other limits: those delineated in the dynamics of power within the social and political spheres that impose their values of identity and behavior on the subject, who then reproduces and/or resists, consciously and unconsciously, the form. Kelsey's prose emphasizes the destructive dynamics of the engrained gender binary as she considers what, beyond the recursive rigidities of the sex-gender system, can create conditions of liberation. One has the sense that she is attempting a kind of magic through negative critique—a critique that would redirect energies from the death drive back into the pleasure principle. Toward this, in profuse endnotes, she refers to the work of powerful women artists and intellectuals—from Ana Mendieta to Pina Bausch to second-wave continental feminism and Carrie Noland's theories of the gesture. A note referencing a declaration of the modernist poet Mina Loy startles for its sheer relevance to our current moment of misogyny and patriarchal protectionisms. Kelsey cites Loy's statement that women must "destroy in themselves the desire to be loved" and abandon the need for protection. Women must replace this need with curiosity and courage. Kelsey embellishes Loy's straightforward decree with sensual elaboration:

> Loy's writing floods the mind, becomes a sensation of electrified power coursing under skin, tones of purple-black velvet streaked with garnet and ruby, a combination of softness and serration.

Within the system of Kelsey's work, abundance and limit are constructs that can be joined as well as separated. The intellectual concern for limit and its significant role within the philosophical essay as one of ethical inclusion and openness to the future is addressed in a number of instances including in this note on "choice":

> The experience of "to choose" becomes different from standing before a vitrine saying "I would like to have *this* and *this* and *this*. Or nothing here is good enough for me." It cascades, a process of interaction, a gesture *toward*, which is always entwined with its substance…

One cannot discuss this text without making a note that the prominent word "sphere" implicates a conceptual scheme of non-identity as it crosses between disciplines and knowledge systems. The domestic sphere is not the same realm as the atmosphere, and yet they are entwined in a fashion that, if recognized, could change one's feeling of relation to the world. The work is arranged under the subheadings of the four earthly subsystems, "Geosphere," "Biosphere," "Atmosphere," and "Hydrosphere," to which are added the "Celestial Sphere" and interludes of more fragmented, poetic language titled "Cosmogony." These subheadings along with the cosmological variant key into the interpenetrating realms of Kelsey's most critical interests.

"Interlayer" is another term she deploys in order to instantiate the connections among violence, ecological destruction, the garden of earthly delights, and the desiring systems of life-world or habitus—which is constituted by the particular physical and abstract spaces of Being and the modes through which a person reflects on these. The actual places of Kelsey's habitus are numerous and include the Eastern United States countryside, the cosmopolitan city, parts of Eastern Europe, the childhood bedroom, and the valleys and farmlands of her native Southern California. A striking passage placed in this region demonstrates Kelsey's consciousness of the interlayer as it is construed in colonial violence, linguistic community, agri-business toxins, man-made water systems, and historical and geological matter:

> Because interlayered I cannot break fish from pesticide, cannot break *Iviatim* from *Cahuilla*, Salton Trough from San Andreas Fault, agricultural drainage reservoir where Imperial and Coachella valleys meet.

*Of Sphere* is a remarkable contribution to the essay as form in its commitment to the most writerly and experimental potentials of modern and contemporary feminist literature and art. In its address to the pressing ecological problems of the present and its refusal of reductive answers, it is a work of critical curiosity and admirable courage:

> What if instead of a mathematical puzzle with an answer, we considered a problem as a promontory, a headland, a landscape you've woken to realize might be approached in a number of ways.

– Carla Harryman

PROEM: *INTERACTIONS OF SPHERES*

At the Salton Sea or eastern coal towns
and midway on the stair or in Central Park
or Bucharest between light and dark
each gem-like Orthodox church its anti-
concrete morning insists on solitude, what
remains. Or in Midwestern cul-de-sacs
I understood lingering, the right-hand self
devoted to architecture the left-hand self not
devoted to anything at all as what remains

fissures stone embankments, scatters salt
over ice to make a little future to refer to
walking over frozen rivers mind alternating
like an eagle, one eye watching as the other
points to the sky waning, wanting because
what a possession the feather-armor of eagles
they seem never to be cold or to long for July
as I long for the fondly phrased dog days
of summer, Caesar's birth, spring lambs sold
at market before the 1st. As if distant heat
might make sense of interior's glittering icons

one body nestles to the side of another
become animal even as the lyric figure revolving
the mind's eye for some reason, for no reason
costumed Pre-Raphaelite is led to the cliffs
musked and bound but still so devoted as if
light's heart had just broken against its glass
bridge lights tinseling blue river hue because yes
even now I aestheticize you I aestheticize loss—
soft murmurs of being-animal cannot save us.

# OF SPHERE

"…to understand dung chemically and spiritually and with the earth sense, one must first understand the texture, spiritual and chemical and earthy of the rose that grows from it."

– H.D. *Notes on Thought and Vision*

# GEOSPHERE I

Our house dismantled, I weave myself deep into countryside fields, roots, stones, searching for traces of lost animality while you spend day after day in a museum looking at, rather than through, windows as if in a window museum. And then looking out of, rather than at, paintings as if they reveal a journey with you in the lead, I behind, your daughter with her dog trailing at the back. I don't blame you, for a sense of home, of ground, might figure as a globe charm suspended from a child's heirloom bracelet worn long after the favorite ribbon was folded and stored in a little gilt box. And the trees near leaflessness increasingly unable to hide the power poisonous berries give to bald light. As eyeglasses extend our eyes do we understand ourselves as figures in a triptych, actor and actress hypothesizing apocalypse, enacting apocalypse, ending in a shock of white?

Such forces, unspeakable, structure conventions of who can I call, are you free to talk though it's Tuesday with our standing at the sink eating quick breakfast and no time for the dog's hurt paw or careful backing down the drive. I admit to expecting answers from the number of butterflies, orange and blue, swarming where the house had been. From our Airstream parked at the periphery I wait for a sign: should we rebuild in grand manner or caravan bohemian away? They swarm, creating an image of your lapels, my pearls strung over lace. We flicker in the field as if wanting to be photographed.

Is the pronoun "we," then, to become little else than acquiescence to inherited flight pattern, circadian clock, position of sun in the sky? This isn't the way we intended to make decisions, "you" the sensate blur of touching in the dark, unsettling sight's certainty as pretending to be wind through goldenrod "I" aspires to a form of clarity streaked with berry juice and running naked through tall grass.

This differs from the take-it-all view: after dismantling the house at the edge of the field the aboveground pool is all that's left, ladder leading up, slide leading down. The groundcover roses approximate weeds, emanate as you practice the script again and again turning on your heel to perfect the walk-away—*Fort! Da!*— though we both know the bus station's too far to reach by foot. With each cue I gape as if slapped while still admiring your finesse, pea coat with matching felt hat.

If the mandate was *return* why take the most painful path? Bramble-out, the last time we ventured this way we were on horseback and so the sweeping vista was to-be-taken. Now I've arrived by car, occupied with clouds rushing east until looking down I recognize the robin body, entrails ruby. Dirt path the dream had not been like this, had spiraled into statuette with no parental imprint, no social order, no etching of experience away. To be made instead a little effigy of self inscribed on the bone cover of a pocket watch. Imitation antique on display in an exhibit about whaling, environment, and abuses of colonial power.

# GEOSPHERE II

You sit in the coatroom checking and rechecking your phone while the dancing begins outside under globe lights. We arrived here together but only externally, which is why in dreams I wake cold, wanting to dance, planning the periphery of a garden laced with continual blooms produced in Denmark. I concede to the nesting texture of camel-hair coats, leather, brocade cape giving way to nostalgia for grandfather's cigar-smoked study and so perhaps I should call you from Paris, which is what we call the patio. I could pretend to be the Fawn producing old-fashioned English-style blooms, soft pink in such absolute profusion they completely cover their own mid-green foliage, so let us dance.

So let us dance for it would be difficult to disguise the voice of someone who has actually begun dancing. If the scene is set liquidly we will come upon the party by noticing first shadows on the lawn and then differentiating orchestration from what the owls do. Or coming upon something floral as leaves shake gold and bronze. Nature viewed as a shop getting ready to close, the street asserting itself against the notion it might as well not exist if existence is to be useful to commerce, that is to say, to subject-formation and point of view. I might be shallow, or perhaps just primal, but I love the blooms.

I love because a phrase, heard before, cradles. But what's the point if one is to be just a statuette fitted so nicely in the palm of a hand? And you, preferring to stand outside the scene as if someone appointed you keeper of the terrarium, clutching your interlocutor close in the glow of your phone. I exaggerate, but what else to make of your story where the chick's pushed from its nest, not yet dead when insects begin their devouring?

Dancing was much easier when it commenced in formal fashion. A thick black line formed by men in proper dress, women unfurling their floral. And thus I could have been the Fawn in dusty rose with private knowledge of thong and peek-a-boo bra hinted by the shock of pheasant hair plume. But we don't live in such a time and talk to each other internally, communicating remarks by text message and gesture as we walk down the mall. I would like to have *this* and *this* and *this*. Or nothing here is good enough for you.

When you point toward the trees asking after my favorite I understand this as a test. Because what is not to like about a tree? This one willows as if longed for. This one flames out, nonplussed. And the Magritte trees lining the periphery begin so very slowly their suburban illumination.

# GEOSPHERE III

Because we must navigate both forward and backward I pause at a description of the little desk. Antique with chipped white paint, ink well, drawer with lock, key strung around my neck for years and then somewhere, lost. Imagining a scene such that it will overtake memory, far strains of a song, sister's damp hand as she jimmies the lock. Here a devotion to materiality strides in before turning, as when matching paint we must decide if the color should blend with what has been weathered. Or should we correspond to the object we once had been? Written at the world's beginning then cut down, grafted back up, cut down, grafted back up. Here flower, there follower, I seem to be commanded of rivers whose orchestration doesn't entail the dancer's sway and dip, but if you take my hand we'll accomplish some form of awkward grace.

Or we might begin with day breaking across itself. Earthen with a Freudian *is*. I am. You are. The camera follows a sequined shoe flung into the river and I come to speak from a position of diving-after. Up to my waist in murky water then plunge and then up. To no avail. Like moths flinging themselves into lamplight we vilify uncertainty until there's no longer any connective tissue left. Which means we begin with mistake, turquoise let in only along edges, the day only along slats of mini-blinds. I pull the cord and someone like me speaks into too-blue air.

My entrance hesitant: not as in I had no idea or longing to impart but knuckle-bare and holding on to reins for dear life. This, even if decked out in rhinestones and prom-blue taffeta which perhaps I should be embarrassed by but a lone bird crying into rain, sycamore infested with squirrels, we don't always command what we wear. As a method for comprehending the animal world I distrust statistical data but follow your experiments with more than moderate imagination. I'm entranced by your period of sitting before still lifes, oysters shucked and exuding, lemon touched to test quivering and then undone with little forks. This, compared to time-lapse photos of retrograde motion, Venus appearing at first to be caught coursing backwards through sky and then, upon reconsideration, creating the illusion of stasis upon the moved.

Which did nothing to augment the dancing, but in all honesty these small gatherings feel as if they take place not under globe lights but as some philosopher's *bildungsroman* presented before a presidential tree. At one with the audience we watch the sun traverse, nothing celebratory in fighter jets passing, echelon formation. This is not a choice location from which to understand the self, complete only after it surfaces into the world. We are sure of this but have yet to propose an alternative: what other world, what other manner of surfacing? In some situations the possessive just doesn't ring true though under certain constellations I want to be the dumb beast shivering with breath and sweat beneath your body. Our condition must be a result of too little dancing, too much pretending to be the Fawn, too much listless floating in the aboveground pool unattached, as it is, to any house.

# GEOSPHERE IV

I return without you to the museum, sit before the painting of your little pink daughter unfolding in time, born first a sack of blood and soft bones then aging into a four year-old who matches her mother, though her mother always wears gray. It's not difficult to analyze such an image. They sit in a public square defined as an aspect of time, mother and daughter surrounded by trees depicted between October and November. We're strangers except for our participation in this moment, the three of us slightly more gold than we otherwise would have been, folding into the fountain, the cloud of the mother's skirt.

Then falling into the mother-dress I'm still singular but blurred with humidity, consciousness held by a scorpion clamped at the base of her-my skull, poison ready to knot down her-my neck. Metallic singing river bugs. This condition of pain cannot be soothed by fennel but we long to become fennel nevertheless, which is as close as the mother-dress ever comes to wanting to dance. Drawn to your little pink daughter I was not her mother but our hair was painted with the same shock of white.

On the ground beneath us: a tiger-skin rug, head with glass eyes, mouth open to reveal teeth. We exist as part of the public square, fountain in the center, kids zooming by on scooters, mothers talking on phones, on benches eating lunch sit the fathers of sons and daughters who attend other parks. An airplane drifts slowly above. Trees project their lace and I, no longer able to fall into the mother-body, fall into the tiger. It was stun dart then fur heavy-cradled onto the mattress on the floor. And a soft night spread until I was revealed, like this, to the public square.

This is collective interior and no amount of effort could tear me from looking. My body feline wanting dank mattress and sex even as the scorpion clamps, muscles knotting down my neck, fountain sparkling out. As the mother-body floats away I hold onto your little pink daughter by the knot at the back of her sash. An interior condition, the ascenders and descenders of letters lift, feathers in the trees, the dress soft with humidity.

# GEOSPHERE V

Visual imagery reveals our habits of belief: lantern-like flowers compose English sentences while fuchsias depreciating in soil thrive on fish emulsion. Which perhaps accounts for the quiet gold hurt although it was only leaves pulling light through windows. You don't need to tell me you intend to depart for the city while the afternoon's still new: it would be stupid to wait for this meadow's permission, sulky mud embedded with animal bones. And so over your shoulder a long view can be retained by a glance: a glass globe surrounding birds, stars, gods. A glass globe surrounding cornfield and aboveground pool, rangy weeds where the house had been.

Some of these objects are by experience confirmed: birds, stars, pool. And some disconfirmed: gods, the taste for formal dance carried off by music pouring from open windows of the biker bar, studded leather jacket and dog collar replacing taffeta and tulle though the thong and peek-a-boo bra maintain the same appeal. I understand: we only come to awareness when the familiar world recedes. In dream the bell continues, the ring it makes upon the hour always attended, held until its fade. I suppose this will have to suffice for the day's release regardless of my desire to rut in the field before we part.

Yes, society's distorted reflection often creates pain, but denial of self-reflection means both social and physical death. This is the way one ascends to the status of imaginative object: the turquoise pendant so light one might forget one was holding it in one's hand. And so with a gesture flung into the meadow when I meant merely to indicate the location of the aboveground pool, its water green but swimmable. This particular variety of painting is now extinct but the work itself still lives, never accosted by switchblade or flame. And its viewer changed only in external presentation: reeds woven into her-my hair, rib cage a terrarium for plants grown from the center of the earth.

# COSMOGONY

                            a gesture insists
on repeating: dying moth     tiny crystal bell
glitter swirled around Statue of Liberty
in her     snow globe

                            left a video
of a woman walking through her house
it's all I could offer     re-film the film
from her point of view

                                    small camera
            strapped to my forehead     electronic
coronet
                        where she paused     sails
            in wind   worn corduroy     lover's
            warm palm

                    the consequence
of relation depends on outline     blossom
inlayed in cement
                    eyes closed:     lawn
mower     refrigerator     airplane

                        eyes open:
house torn from body
ivy from walls     building flung become
a temple in the sky
                        earth ground into
sand     this was all


                                    my mind a center of quartz

                            trees     screen the river     pitch
                            pine     tamarack     ash     gesture

each place a delicate golden cage
                                immutable
trout shimmer
                rotted river grass
a knife-slash releases plastic beads from
the fish's gut
                and the trees     the animals
bow down


                                the day carrying
                                        a blown-out robin's egg
                        so little upon which     we agree

                        the beach last June not quite warm
                        enough for swimming

                                        speaking with you
                        on the phone once provided     solace
                        now only grief     occipital lobe nearly

                        melting     what comes before     with
                        softness away

                                        until each day the hollow
                        of a vessel

                                        so sea becomes cloud
                    becomes rain    becomes sea
                    variation cycling: what is world shifts


                        sky gods overriding
lyric interludes    thigh's soft flesh

acanthus leaf from its column broken
placed in a museum    becomes artifact

tucked into backpack    appropriation
climbing out of the skylight


                                        camera switched off
                        shoulder blades pressed together
                        play at having wings

                                    my body might arc
                        through layers of smog and cloud

                        speed dust    into dust

# HYDROSPHERE I

We apprehend the train through its whistle, but is it a mistake to understand a thing by the way it cries itself into existence? Light openings come upon us inhaling particles so newly hewn from earth we become more earth, more elemental to the system of organic and inorganic machines. In response to the stained-glass transom feel ruby and amber melt into skin, line the box with velvet for shards because fragility, too, sustains us. And so hum with me into care for the town's balsa-wood model and rabbit's foot. Dollhouse to rented Victorian, window opening that held a shimmering peacock replaced by plate glass.

And so discern the truth of frost soon to come upon the room's silence and hooked rugs. I had planned for more than sitting across from a stranger with my eyes closed. And then enter the child and she tore the quiet from us, for we had become accustomed to reading internally, fingertips run along the impressions of letter-pressed text and so words coursing through course up.

In this way we aren't restricted to the totality of arrival, our skin compared with other animals, relatively thin, but under: the sinews, the organs, the bones. Identifying with the floodwall you make a circling action with your hands. I, having become a woman whose gestures are orchestrated by such a house, make a paper crane, tuck it into the bodice of my dress. Which is to neglect to ask you how you feel about the words rolling around in both of our mouths well-knowing that the absence of question indicates having been dragged back from audience rustle, rabbit letting out a small gasp before darting to its hedge. The phrase misremembered until enough leaves fall for the view to startle, thought come upon us, exposure the first condition of becoming a thing crying itself into existence. By mint patch and chain link you offered me this.

By habit we fling seeds to populate the dirt between slaughterhouse and monument, for otherwise who could bear to inhabit such a place? In the rural version homesteads ghost beneath ivy, the law of traversal drawing me to you through timothy and switchgrass. When we ask the child to sketch a line between true and false she encloses both terms in a circle. We build from this, sometimes beginning with the fluidity of gesture, connection of stone to mind then words unhinge, writing wind rushing into my mouth made of me a rabbit trap.

Which has little or nothing to do with whether or not a defunct coal town appeals to a contemporary audience. When I ask after your trips to the city you make a cutting gesture to indicate reason. I finger the nub of quartz in my pocket to indicate home. The river eases back from its floodline revealing inscription only accessed from a distance. As in standing opposite the town's balsa-wood model in order to declare the sentence complete. Gold trinkets sliding out of their cardboard box.

# HYDROSPHERE II

Lest you forget, the town will remind you: you are not a god. You are not an enlarged self. You are not even a whole self. The day came upon us dousing the tapestry with light, lemon tree in one corner symbolizing salvation, in the other a dog for fidelity. In the rural version I drive to the path above the river and walk the dog. And only upon driving back into town do I notice the line of the river receded, dead fish on the banks, for I couldn't afford my own state of being, the crawling out that it entails dependent on the floodwall holding. The child divides true from false and then encircles them, thought come upon us, then clearing, coffers possessing nothing but debt.

The relation was to the text and only to the text. But now add rain hitting windows, work trucks paving the road before dawn, vibrations moving sinew and bone. An object in a series of objects I've fallen into construction light streamed through the room to shine upon a photograph of a woman in the desert, water pitcher balanced on her head. And then cradled, then elongating her arm she walks away from the temple trailing a jagged path. Affect as a layering of intensity and then the cessation of intensity. Longing, then fingertips on a cuff, on your wrist.

To meet in the doorway face to face does not portend the barn fire, horse cornered in its pen, nostrils steaming. Does not portend the foundations exhumed when they readied the site for construction, cloisonné fingerbowl holding orange rind, globe charm, a swatch of red flannel. I look into your eyes for this. Tipped into fire and so sparked and then tranquil, the effects of breathing such a smoke.

Or scattered into wind to no avail because I do this standing on the bow of the boat sowing seed from hand as if ash, and to ash, for after wedding machine to earth we can no longer consider ourselves immune. Gasses seep from chambers deeply embedded in rocks to create visions of sea grass crowning the hill, the name you awaken, uttering.

# HYDROSPHERE III

In the pause between storms we're hand and hand through the public garden bedded down at winter's edge. What happens when landscape erodes beyond recognition, its name a ribbon of text embedded in my skin? Pulse there. Vein there through plate glass and iron railing, the abandoned patio and beyond, the road, and beyond, the mall, but more often than not I'm wrong about the detail, the citation, the text. For example, the remnant of a rose grafted to the action of tying a stone to the dog then pushing her under. For example, when we look up we see the pink cloud overtaking the yellow. Beyond this our narrative displays a refusal to acknowledge the gash of light, skywriter's script, anabatic wind stopped singing. At the mouth of the cave the terracotta pitcher grown heavy in my arms.

The prospect of becoming more than just a text embedded in orange rinds flung into fire before the wooden steeple, utmost quiet. The marble statue must be carved and cannot be cast, cannot, therefore, be multiplied. As opposed to Russian thistle, tumbleweed. Are we each unique and therefore irreplaceable or are we multiple, encountering the many ways one might be consumed?

When standing alone sound teases from sound until singing's detected under the electric saw, swallows beneath the underpass, sibilance beneath the knife time will use to scratch out our names. The audience shifts in her chair, breathes alternating vibrations as I open the box and find a miniature galleon, a matchstick doll in a lace dress for the crow's nest, a matchstick doll in a flannel vest for the helm.

As an ode to the Law of Similarity and the Law of Contact, pierce the eye of the doll and your enemy is blind; pierce the stomach and she is sick; pierce the head and her head aches; pierce the breast and her breast will suffer the dream wherein I whisper into your sleeping ear: A true husk / led me to dwell with you inside the house. / A true husk / led me to dwell with you in the present tense. / In this way / we came to fall / through the firmament.

So in this manner come to meet oneself, run into oneself in mirrors, struggle with one's double, love oneself in them while hating oneself, project oneself while losing oneself in facticity, a paper bird, a styrofoam bird, a shot thing with lead in its belly but nevertheless one-two-three beats of the wing. And so over the retaining wall tinsel simulates flight. This I bring to the sum of whispers permeating our night-dark room. To how I imagine your face in sleep, your skin not flesh but scales, your gently sweating brow.

# HYDROSPHERE IV

To take a chisel to marble and release the poppy with its petals still intact. A set of wings and a floodwall. Lion mask. Yet what was inside, interior, didn't exist before carving, polished bowl of an empty room, salt-washed skull, bee trapped under glass. Or devoted to the train approaching and the push of its whistle through air, syllable-meld with the scrape of iron on iron, emplaced echoing. Or inside the nautilus a testimony of self-to-self: you regret turning away when he turned away. You regret driving upriver as if what mattered most was not revelation, not petals falling to reveal in the center—what? Stamen, insect, light? But instead becoming one with the machine steadily bearing you north, turquoise never-end below.

And so closing the Victorian pocket doors to volumes of outside wind. To the postcards of Le Corbusier's *Unite d'habitation* aligning itself with the window view—abandoned patio, iron railing, road to the mall, the hill beyond. Enclosed in a shell, a hull, a pod case integument shuck glowing in Low German *huske*, little house, two candles refracted in a hurricane glass. And so embark: a doll for the crow's nest. A doll for the helm. And we sail into the glow of the digital clock.

As opposed to looking for a stone to tie to my wrist. Then looking for a glass to angle light in so as to strike a fire while standing in the town center saying "I heretofore make myself subservient to this" and thus become historical, a small woman all in blue, the hem of my dress ablaze. Viewed from a balcony above the valley of the cross, oak banister etched with sun disk, pentagram, eternal knot, the wound still tastes of salt, the body's delicate down heightened by first a ruby light, then amber plunge. And all along a future narrator crouched behind the granite outcrop, listening.

From the bluff we consider the last storm's damage a stripping-off of architecture the land can no longer use. Branches ignited, and for a moment I illuminated the world, which is to say, I illuminated a little circle of stalemate. Position pierced the eye, pierced the stomach, pierced the head, pierced the breast, pierced the shoulder. And lobbed the ostrich-feathered dummy bird beyond the hedge. And so falling through the firmament the insubstantial becomes a plunging stone. Shutters clasped against another rain.

Through the doorway light falls as she-I bend down, wide neck of her-my blouse slipping, shoulder wound, leather's weal. He will touch her-my shoulder or he will not. The building appropriated by use and by perception, by touch and by sight, by home, cannot be understood in terms of the attentive concentration of a tourist before the Parthenon. Which is not the same as under the illuminated steeple we cast our rinds into the fire pit, and then our map, fingers singed with too-late-to-pluck-it-out.

# HYDROSPHERE V

We should not forget that by giving the king's daughter the clue to the labyrinth the architect ordains the minotaur's death. We go to the top of the bluff to practice vision, road and floodwall following the river's curve. The alternate route we memorize before dark, metallic rain on wet wood filing air. What your lips say contradicts what your tongue says and what your teeth say is different from the poem whose words wake from the sleeping porch surrounded by hissing trees, bradawl, scratch awl, stitching awl.

I approach the landscape by identifying the word for "and," the word for "here," for "there," the ending that signifies something plural saying "ssss" when I see the letter "s." In this I find a beginning: how many ways to say it still rains, while using the logic of Ariadne's thread you calculate and recalculate the force of pressure accruing at the crest gate. The dog has not walked more than a one-block radius for days, door swollen and shoulder against and lean and even then a resistance to exiting, entering, house sealing itself up. A seed pod, battened hatch, subject to be forced open, poured out.

You regret touching her-my shoulder or you do not, for she was and was not me, just as you are and are not my beloved, our mouths engorged with petal and thorn. But you say "I" as if there were a marble figure buried under flesh who regrets cutting the lace dress off the matchstick doll, regrets lashing her to the bow of the boat, heavy with accumulated water turning each object that it touches into stone. Such as the bucket, such as the pitcher, such as the skirt of my dress and shoes filled and wet wool. Yet at a certain point water in movement renders objects light, an overflowing that makes so little of trees in its wake, the town in the face of this force become true to its balsa-wood model.

From the balcony above the labyrinth I find I am not the daughter of the king. I'm the interpreter and don't know what to make of near-flooding or the graffitied wall that stayed the bulk of water. And how to read our kneeling on the riverbank next to dead crayfish and we cried there, rubbing mud into arms and chests.

I approach the text to learn whether or not I will be spared the headache, stomachache, shoulder wound. I approach the text to see how quickly I become trees uprooting sidewalks, abandoned sportswear factory, chapel's milk-glass windows, patterns tightening in service of a discourse that does more than deposit linguistic layers. Does more than archive, than testimony the body withdrawn, text of the nail rusted in and found the Queen of Spades in the mud along with a plastic crucifix.

As *we* you and I slip in and out of retrospect. We regret stoning the stained-glass window even as our arms shiver ecstatic with its crash. We do and do not regret transplanting the heirloom rose thereby reinstating your lineage. We regret navigating absence with retribution but don't regret the braying sighs of make-up sex lingering through "Good morning" and "How nice the bud vase" and "The dog's already been taken out." Amidst such pleasantries you stand watching a boy bury a mouse to its neck and I, part-mouse part-boy, also stand watching, regretting only the lost camera as I focus my cinematic eye. You say "I wanted, I want." I say "I was, I am," creating text as excrescence even as the self continues proliferating in excess of the view giving onto the patio with its wrought-iron railing and beyond, the road, and beyond, the wall.

# COSMOGONY

the I-you
            photograph     river cut

becomes     a little sun above horses
driven north     not enough
time     for coats to fur
                        to thread
ourselves with phrase
                        body a theater
presencing before spring


                            but perhaps     together
            we create nothing at all     crystallize
            separate thoughts     void within     void
            without winter

                            the world suddenly
            unalloyed     longing to soften
            into earth

                                   into wind's    *yes* then *null-*
                         *null* over vinyl siding


I understood:     river splitting
past the nuclear power plant

                                   we've been
trying to order chaos all along     rows
of yellow peas bred with green called
out    *yellow*     as each plant began
to fruit

          I not saying     but thinking:
this experiment
                         tip of an arrow     *yellow*
primordial carcass carved     a continent
performed before

                but as the site alters     I alter
the local body     my body     the place
of that body     my place     red
thread

            to late winter snow     dog pulling
toward the river     piles of rock resolve
into wings     long necks     heads tucked
to plump bodies

                        four geese frozen
on the bank     as if the mind had a core
of ice

the house    shingles off    mortar
thinning to sand    opens to an image
pried from unmediated flow:

as I sleep
a woman lifts my head from the pillow
gathers my hair    cuts it short with
a pocket knife


the *I*    then    an attempt
red lacquer box    little dragon inlaid
in jasper and jade    two windows    rattan
blinds


fragment of landscape the ground
caved    swallowed our house    I stood
in the park and watched

# BIOSPHERE I

To begin with an internal phrase: *This is the world as it exists coursing through me.* Language says this, comes upon me in the east overlooking a winter garden, steeple, Pennsylvania coal breaker back mountain horizon. Snow overlayering last summer we replanted his mother's heirloom rose transplanting origin, a season of eyes closed sunstaining lids to poppy-poppy stamen lash.

Flicker-image, eyes open I woke in winter, mind running west to the Pacific and my native California. Homeland, origin panning in from the coast to the Salton Sea populated with images of abandoned motorboats, petrified fish, buildings pulled by sand into sand, structures calling to mind Lee Bontecou's canvas-stretched steel constructions. Images mark this, come upon me digging hands into coarse-ground shells lifted to my mouth but then I'm moving out to a Google-eyed view of seismic graph and aerial vista, sea transformed into turquoise gash, devotional object underlayering the screen as it brings the world to hand.

And thus the *I* the world courses through fills with landscape, culture, sensation. Fills with a white colt sealing the horizon with a bolt-run along the edge, valley in smoke below. The mind disperses with birds flying out of the skull of a woman under a tree in blue taffeta waiting for visions past midnight. She-I had done some digging, we touched humus and worm, our hours spent not asleep return as dropped coins, as reverse hibernation, the dead communicating via radio static. Thrush in the hand and then a white silk handkerchief providing a light source from within. A white nearly silver. Our hand so white it is nearly silver.

And the beach of crushed fish bones much more coarse than sand because untouched by waves, the inland sea for decades unmoved as pelicans, egrets, grebes flock up, dive down. Or should I say seemingly unmoved because continually fed by runoff: onion, sweet corn, Bermuda grass treated with malathion, carbaryl, pyrethroids while at the same time the shoreline recedes markedly, slowly, evaporation simultaneous with seeping because bodies eventually absorb, resolve into other elements. Following the path of difference between accidental and intentional causation taffeta frays, hem wet, hands smelling of fish long after they're washed. World to animal, animal to earth moved remarkable in salinity, in pollution, how can any living thing wash up on this shore?

# BIOSPHERE II

A two-minute video clip charts the centuries of cycles drying out and flooding to thus create the Salton Trough, birth an accidental sea. A meandering flute backs the voiceover goddess History sealing the river's mouth. Or History as a gesture from falconry stitching closed the eyes of the hawk, old maps labeling the valley *Cahuilla*, the Spanish name for the tribe whose endonym, *Iviatim*, was erased with the rise of the missions. Bodies eventually absorb, dissolve, move from accident to intention back to accident.

Because interlayered I cannot break fish from pesticide, cannot break *Iviatim* from *Cahuilla*, Salton Trough from San Andreas Fault, agricultural drainage reservoir where Imperial and Coachella valleys meet. To wait under a tree at midnight wanting to see like H.D. *writing on the wall*, images cast on a screen. A head in profile, a chalice, a ladder, an angel called Nike. To name as a form of knowing while at the same time understanding some names efface, close out the white colt as if it had never been. As if *Iviatim* had never been.

At a down-thrust angle diving for prey the Goddess of Victory, origins Egyptian and/or Phoenician, speeds back towards the valley as light splits over the conquistador, braid of thorns unlacing my summer dress, shoulders exposed to raw moon, back to earth, field fallow I have yet to develop a conversational voice to talk myself out of wilderness. Instead: when not balancing mid-studio recovering from this balance, standing at a window, paused in a doorway, painting at an easel, writing at a desk. We hold our brush with the posture of a scribe of future weather wherein the radio floats through an open window giving Nike a body of earth, prismatic wings.

But do we need a prophetess to tell us that when the Salton Sea dries up veils and veils of toxins, sea floor dust, will release over Southern California coating crops, palms, cars, lawns, swimming pools static with pesticide? But what if we could save the sea by carving a channel to the Pacific, a flood of reciprocal waters, desert greening with southern magnolia and rugosa, coast to inland transposed? An Eden fantasy, sister to the Technicolor kitsch of '60s postcards depicting the Salton Sea as inland resort. Backed by a turquoise Corvette flanked by two palms, in a red bathing suit I squinted into the sun. Vacation here. A projection layering crushed fish bones creates a new series of gestures, hand on my hip, head tossed back, the internal action of kissing the turquoise pendant that reminds me of home and then casting it into the sea.

# BIOSPHERE III

When we think of the self as being alongside, contiguous, we understand ourselves to be separate but also positioned so as to touch. As in the three dialects of *Cahuilla*, of *Iviatim*: dialect of Desert, of Mountain, of Pass. And when we think of the self as adjacent we admit to a different relation: we don't touch but are connected by having nothing else of our kind between. As in *Nike*, the Greek word meaning "victory," rooted in *Neikos*, "quarrel and strife," adjacent to *Nekht*, ancient Egyptian word affixed to the names of Pharaohs embodying the falcon-headed sky god Horus, meaning "strong," "peerless," "divinely blessed." Yet, while both words are similar and evoke wings, *Nike* and *Nekht* are etymologically independent and distinct. Thus within a house rooms with shared walls are contiguous to one another, but we say the adjacent church. The adjacent mall. The street between at times so difficult to cross.

In parallel, the veil between past and present thins, a transparency evident in objects such as the to-scale replica of Athena Parthenos standing not in Athens but within the concrete reproduction Parthenon in Nashville, Tennessee. There she poses in gold helmet, stark blue eyes, gold necklace, gold dress, with a six-foot golden Nike in her outstretched palm. But as I enter her chambers I nevertheless weep, not for the emptied temples of the Acropolis, but for the story sculpted on the Parthenon's frieze.

Thought for centuries to celebrate a civic parade honoring Athena, the frieze culminates above the temple's eastern door in the figures of a woman with two girls along with a man and a child holding a piece of cloth previously assumed by classicists to be the goddess's sacred golden dress. In the twenty-first century the depiction transforms when its story is discovered on papyrus strips used for Egyptian mummification. The scraps reveal 250 lines of a lost play by Euripides dramatizing this same scene. This is not just any family, but King Erechtheus, his wife, and his three daughters. And, the royal family is not on their way to just any parade. Rather, mother, father, and three daughters prepare the youngest for sacrifice; the piece of cloth not Athena's dress, but funerary linen unfolded, the girl's death intended to save Athens from defeat.

A stilled figure is considered to be an object until she begins speaking, released to her body in this way. To learn this is to recall we used to think of the self as aura, body overflowing its dress. Like her Nashville doppelgänger, phantom, clone, the ancient Athena was also constructed around a wooden frame, her robe made of gold until removed, melted down in order to pay Athenian soldiers, then replaced by bronze. An object becomes figurative when it overflows intention, wakes stuttering and thirsty to the sound of geese, the window a form to push through, boats overturned in snow.

Do you continue to need the name of the valley when you inhabit the valley? Your imagined body reclining there half asleep beneath a date tree, description fused to wilderness as pronouns shift into third person turning self into object, into a *she*, the pendant just cheap enamel but its turquoise color had reminded her of the car in the postcard. The coastline contemplated from a California bluff. The gash in a satellite photograph.

# BIOSPHERE IV

The only time we move in constant curves is in the womb, foetus twisting to the right. The external body, symmetrical, advances linear, looks online at an image of the Nashville Athena undergoing renovation. To consider the screen with a sensation of stepping through code and scaffolding to unwrap the plastic protecting Athena's alabaster chest. Neither accident nor intention we are a complexity of placement, of place, we are this, beveled into an imagined film, *Night of the Living Statue*, Athena stumbling out of the Nashville Parthenon through Centennial Park, traversing Lake Watauga in five easy paces. The goddess marches through town splintering strip malls in her wake as Nike becomes a swoosh adorning the bodies of athletes mid-flight. Tennis skirt. Running shoes. Becomes a surface-to-air defense missile shooting up, flaring out.

To dive from the height of a plane toward turquoise expanse rushing up. To inhabit a pronoun as time limit, two minutes of looking and the image travels through eyes, mind, body and her posture is my posture, her expression my expression. Rose as rose, limit as limit, mountain as mountain.

This is the world as it exists coursing through me, inhabited not by naming but by refusing to talk my way out of wilderness. Language becomes digging fingers into mane, taffeta bunched over hips, thighs gripping a palomino back a-run along the valley ridge. As if we might succeed in siphoning the Pacific into the Salton Sea to save the sea, fish carcasses softening. To create a likeness underpaint skin with green earth made by adding a small amount of black to yellow ocher. Body internal-knowing that if the sea dries out the basin will lift, veil after veil dusting ocean to dull metal.

But what about alternative forms such as atonality or walking into the kitchen and making a slow gesture with my right hand, thereby drawing the angle of light as I remember it coming through the studio's factory windows, the up-swell of piano in its wilderness phase? As if in response the garden is covered with snow and when I attempt to remember the color of the rose I end up at an inland sea, sand of salt and fish bones. To become warm from the desire for warm air through an open window as the day gives itself to conversation between the sick waters of the sea and a single balanced position from which, like Isadora Duncan before the Parthenon, 1921, you cannot know whether you'll next run off stage, move into yet another position, or, even, begin to float. What it means to touch each eye with the first and second fingers, to draw out a Horus line.

To draw an external projection of an internal act, kissing the turquoise pendant, then tossing it into the sea. The path from the mind to the wall is direct, requires waiting under the tree, leafless, salt-smoothed to blue until your body becomes salt-smoothed, blue, crouched in the shell-sand digging through fish bones and then something soft. Was this your heart, your kidney, your eye? Was this my eye, my kidney, my heart?

## COSMOGONY

       orifice    erogenous zone
come to exist through cochineal-dyed

linen    sleeveless    strapless    ankle-
length hem

       twist of hips    bending
to pick somcone else's daughter up

              cold air
pushes warm
       clavicle into shoulder
shivered silver    scanning clouds for
messages
       the coming spring with its
nothing to offer

              the question not of
sex    but of fields    the wheat

did it vernalize
           under all this snow
no telling

so thick with lack the heroine
sacrificed     remains allegorical

through historical atrocity     the house
dependent on what we keep outside

                                        image pried
                        from unmediated flow     meiosis
                        mitosis

                                grackle covering itself in
                        marigold     to rid the parasite


old axis mundi     trunk of the oak
object     for knitting interventions

scarved blue     blossoming

                        might imply nature's
partial to domesticity
                                crown cropped
for power lines

the only time we move in constant
            curves is in the womb
external
bodies    symmetrical
                    carry internal
asymmetry along a straight course


                        transmission towers lattice the desert
                        augur a plane come down
                                        in sand

                        bald Egyptian light
                                        temple pylons
                        construct architectural hieroglyph
                        two hills between which the sun rose
                        and set
                                we pass through

                        you a comet    I ostraca with lotus
                        and winged disk

                                        neither of us lives
                        at the origin anymore

this morning: a stained-glass star
projected    on your forehead

flowers
           sprang from my mouth matter
revealing void    not content

                              whether
or not we'll connect depends on
the arrow nocked to loose: outside

constructed consciousness choice
disintegrates


                              rose so busy keeping up
              her coral color    blooms    and falls
              apart    blooms    and falls apart

# ATMOSPHERE I

The first house of being was at the pier's end, silver planks an untreated structure angling over ocean. There I learned about invisible weather currents, conspiracy of water and air to pull us under not reflected in the seascapes sold beside vendor-booth necklaces of coral and pearl. And so begin at emergency longing like music to advance the root of the shrub as frost etches the garden. Which might or might not delineate the relationship I imagine having with you. Eros, encounter's drift into the ontological not a temporal question outlining where we once lived, but a question of causation and the selves we might release.

And so the first image of the world is overtaken by a second and then a third creates desire's pattern. Not whether or not what we suspect to be true will be documented as true: your skin not flesh but scales, a form of purchasing. Not whether or not you touch my leg under the table to satisfy an extant ideology: your dart not love but sex, a form of giving away. But what does it mean to exist as the flesh of day, cul-de-sac and repeated floor plans offering little direction?

The question then: how to make a self, text, world outside established pattern but familiar enough to read? Rose dug up, root ball wrapped in burlap I approach the town center, not recognized by anyone there. You sit before the fountain with a desire to think beyond what you already know, the boy interior camped at the edge of his mother's garden. The girl interior practices belling her skirt and arms until the body appears to float. As such we began with two ruined languages: the poetic and the philosophical, self and other, beloveds exceeding identity's phrase as music merges through traffic and pigeons. Our proximity conjures mythology: Psyche's blindfold, Eros's quiver and bow, instructions for constructing a snow globe. We'll need a jar, little plastic boat, synthetic evergreen, pair of wings. Distilled water, glitter, glycerin. An after-storm with houses opening out to the streets again, entry into the world each day performed in medias res.

# ATMOSPHERE II

Whereas the world begins in language, the dancer begins in silence. She moves away from words to create phrases with her body, gesture, rhythm. *Away from* and *toward* garnering new import when performed mid-stage in blue, scooping red earth from a pail, running hands over thighs, hips, breasts. This I imitate, looking for instruction because once seen in the mirror the throat's ache struggles to be pronounced out loud. Sparrows littering the lawn flock up as you back the car down the drive. Let us inhabit, not just mouth words on an empty avenue.

And afternoons, walking directly into wind disperses the self over the line dividing neighborhood from meadowland and bluff, freed into thought-gale and eddy. But returning home pragmatics settle in as the desire to create a form for being and then bargain it into existence. Thus the self becomes an image of a woman weaving at the window alone in a long wool skirt. Elegant but anachronistic and bourgeois all the same. Or the self a field of wild poppies, dog curled at my thigh.

Admittedly, this is an attempt to become solid enough to touch, to be longed for. When you appeared I was replacing the question of truth with what can the asking-after show us? That the trees have been heavy with blossom I know with mine own bare eyes revealing the hissing in the dark to have contained vital messages about water and air's conspiracy to pull us under. But before I could attune, all sound was extinguished by your touch. How to move away from the self dictated, which is a question of dissolving the glue holding the image to its cardboard back while the rose, so busy keeping up her coral color, blooms and falls apart.

But there's physical bliss in performing objective sensibility. Throw your voice through the window across the room. Then speak as if unfolding from a transparent plane. I felt but didn't recognize my own body, the height it achieves while leaping, the bell of the skirt, the bell of the arms. This interior presses as we reach the top of the bluff, watch the red-sailed boat waiver at horizon before moving out of sight. Here there is no town center. There is parking lot and restaurant, one hill of trees scaled with lights.

## ATMOSPHERE III

Here's another way of looking at it: I'm on the hunt not only for an original interpretation but for a whole new book of nature, including the balcony's basket of artificial flowers. Let us create a figure for beloveds entwined then released into the space between states of being: were we one or were we two, proposing a logic of slow, refrained, or looped tracks in mud? Or tracks in the glitter-snow structuring body, structuring mind? Hold the camera out the window of a moving car. Take a photograph, terrain in a blur synced with your hand in a blur, invisible things, parts of everything else, determining us.

Or to establish oneself by noticing distance: a red ship makes its way across a red sea, defies a sense of form as fixed position. Because to be married by the glove gives rise to the glove's power regardless that later we cut it to ribbons for the robin's nest. And later yet we turned to the window for a reflective surface, an image of ourselves looking, not so much as a means to secure a sense of self, but how did we materialize as two?

All of which proposes silence, conduit, the pupil of the eye devouring transmission. When I look at the window I see reflected back a figure stripped of age, race, gender. And so project myself upon that vantage, as when in the subway remembering how it feels to take up residence in someone else's interior, Victorian pocket doors, hearth fire. I became as she was, a terrarium with its miniature orange tree, turquoise rocks, and moss.

The day's logic sometimes proposes, as a form for being, the state of sitting in a chair and then standing at the window. Or being as being-seen, live or recorded performances of outward looking. This doesn't entail deleting the awkward photographs: that is a question of choice which, like the nub of quartz in your pocket vibrates with the secret condition of a house dependent on what's kept outside. And then returning to the chair, picking up a book, and watching yourself as if you had split into two bodies. As if one might inhabit one's own double-planetary system.

In fleshing out such circumstances the body itself increases and then diminishes. As in sunflowers finishing their blossom. And so gone to seed in sync with the red ship approaching horizon with its refugees, sailing the border between force and the creation of new expressive forms, expenditure undertaken regardless of debt. "The problem with your language," my beloved said to me, "is that nobody can understand it." The next logical proposition: to move further into collapse, refusing to frame one's life in terms of souvenir landscapes, photographs. To fill the quarry with water overcoming abandoned machinery with a substance that garners its color from the sky.

# ATMOSPHERE IV

Why demand a meadow's silence when what it most insists upon is flung-out desire for blue morphos, rajah, and pasha butterflies? By which I mean to say I had to work so hard at focusing just to see the state of the tree before me because for all our under-the-covers and kissing-your-thistle-burnt-hands, I don't know you. And the tree still leafless but with berries, not in itself so remarkable, but in contrast with the groundcover rose in full bloom I admire its austerity, persistent holding to a winterized body. And we are as transitory as spiders.

Because if spiders don't impulse toward warmth this provides a reason, for in dreams I wake cold. As in circling your name on the list with a red pen. At the same time the meadow's silence creates the concept of quiet-as-mystery. As in a film when the jilted lover mistakes a broken heirloom vase for life becoming somehow more difficult to hold in her shaking hands. We can explain human tenacity in this way: in matter there's a slight list toward being rather than nonbeing. Take standing at the corner in a crowd waiting for the light to change and then suddenly realizing the man in front of you is your lover. And resisting the urge to put your hand on his shoulder, to whisper in his ear "Turn around." Because only in standing behind him can you realize that while he smells of juniper the same as he did when he left the house that morning, you have never before, unobserved, observed him in his natural state.

Yes, inside the window is the person who is now you, looking out. My sister's revelation: seeing him as if he were a stranger allowed me to forget the woman I was trying to be, dressed in blue, born of the horse slowly negotiating a river overcome by ice. Because why else the banner hauled upon the mast but ignorance of its own silk, spider-like stitchery? But rather the moment made focus of the thing that I am. The last pages of a manual on Graham technique. The bell of the skirt and the bell of the arms. As such, we might call to the meadow but cannot commandeer the meadow, as inside the great house the girl commands her toy train. The running of it backward and forward over tracks so satisfying while outside the bridge strung with globe lights carries on. Record set on its turntable. Needle touch and then song.

## COSMOGONY

before drought overtakes
the garden    leaving sky    ocean
wet    yes    yet    such thirst

           the pier's    silver prophecy    untreated
           will disintegrate    I know

                    have known this
           conspiracy of air as    others
           walk the promenade

          Eros slipping
sex throbs through time    a tiger
occupying space

a preference for drowning
shells wrapped    around wrists    self
to sea

sunglasses fill my eyes not with
your eyes    but with sand    sky

city emptying    we become just one
object among
            a democracy of objects

lounging    casual    coconut oil
rubbed    into skin Eros selects
what is grass sharp    salt

                    glass tides knotting the will vs. a theory
                    of the will    a fleet

                    of small white ships    just as any other
                    body might    float I float

                              internal vision
                              a street     lined with orange trees
                              reading by the fountain     weight

                                        a bolt of yellow linen
                              draping shoulders     breasts     hips
                              amplifies the ambient surround


draw you to me as if
                    temple snakes
hissing in my ears     mind's eye pried

draw you to me     as if
the charm of objects     had never
flared out     never clutching at
the statuette

                    goddess eyes turned
inward     pushed me to the temple dirt

right ear    nautilus-pressed
listens to hieroglyphs    long chiseled
from traffic

                such an ordinary day
then ice dropped    into hot coffee
I noticed    never melted    prophecies

the coming flood    bridge too far for
approach by foot    future ache
passing through the body

                body crawling on
its belly    there is no    other way

        the infant toddler clinging
        to her mother's hip    learns the body
        differently than her sister    swaddled

        into a stroller
        wheeled down the promenade

# CELESTIAL SPHERE I

All along the cul-de-sac framed above girlhood beds are posters of Edward Burne-Jones's Psyche on the way to her wedding in funeral attire, led to the cliff to be married off to a monster. Depicted as procession, a sage and nine Pre-Raphaelite women walk past low blue-green mountains, willowy in long dresses they are extensions of landscape, each face the same solemn English rose. Lyre, violin, shawl, and embroidered cuffs as if born part of a banner fluttered from a window. From girlhood beds blooms a subtlety of feeling in excess of Tupperware and sweatsuits, a sensation incorporated into the world continuing on as I write this, re-knotting the tasseled curtain cord I use for a belt.

This conceptualizes you as Eros, myself a Psyche, her blindfold silk, scented with juniper, metaphorical. And so let us look at similarities of lineage: failing to conform through no fault of her own she's taken to the mountain to stand against wings in the night, distant siren, hem torn by wind. Are we actually surprised that outside the system of the house she encounters talons and thorns, silk rip and petal shred?

Desire conjures exaggerated versions of what is longed for, tears petals from daisies to play at making snow, world made fresh and white and, under, fields gather energy. This, loved or loved-not, prophetic in the vacant lot adjacent to the gas station, Adventist church, Taco Bell. But doesn't ardency construct a little grove and demand I wear nothing, stand before the trees in my nudity, oil lamp in my hand?

And so embodiment is realized by seeping feet into earth as from the crown of the head come celestial light explosions, a veil of sparks even when walking down the street in a faux-fur coat and hat or even when, as a dove, one moves from the interior of a cage to its exterior. Such movement currents beneath the *I*, the self culminating in hunger and fullness released as thermal energy acting on oceanic and continental lithospheres, thinning along rift valleys and mid-ocean ridges, tectonic plates shifting.

Reading over my shoulder you say in this day and age tassels sacrifice much-needed sense to sound and play, and I say don't you think sense is something one might usefully tear from reason, hunger back into the body? You say beyond the edges of cul-de-sacs police with riot clubs always have pulled out guns. I say do we know how to make the sound of bravery without talons, *kirschwasser* in our throat, cherries on our tongue? I say this halfway up the stairs, turning as the door closed. Or, I say to the door, we might relinquish sense, move into sound, become the vibration shuddering door into frame into wall into window looking out to a blue-coated figure who gets into his car, departs. *Fort!* And then a boy on a bike. *Da!* And then the neighborhood's lost flock of gulls.

# CELESTIAL SPHERE II

We pull ourselves through ourselves again and again, a line of women walking to the sacrifice, bodies identical, expressions identical. You know me by the lyre in the crook of my arm, the color of my hair. The body furs and bites, mouth alive with eating roses, and so yes I wanted to see you, not just touch you in the dark wondering over the substance and quality of your wings. Certainty falls short and then, with an alteration in humidity, fuses into marble figure. Let us stand at-gaze before the world which is to say before the window, open, day pouring in and both of us naked, here, harshlight crude-pointing at the brute fact of the body, the imperfect body at noon.

I continue the notebook within a language that won't soften as it becomes an object, even under touch. Admitting our late stage of empire we compare ourselves to Rome: during the Hannibalic war it rained stones, a child was born with an elephant's head, in Sardinia two shields sweated blood. We pull ourselves through ourselves again and again. The essence of sacrifice unsatisfied with mere rhetoric demands that writing of the English rose one take up her posture and it is mere steps from this to the cliff. Sound's transmission through bone is the way I explain my attraction to the little grove of elms, mineral-rich water, fish inordinately large surface saying "Take care of Rome" before plunging under.

Would you prefer I turn in narration to celebrate your coming upon me there, the budding-forth before leafing-out, hiking my dress above my waist we fucked, my back against the tree, petals raining down an epithalamium of weather?

Subjection, however, also depends on performativity of rhetoric. If I agree to own you, you become for me mere object, displaced from the category of things that are to be loved. If you agree to own me, etcetera. Light streaming through an ice-glazed window inspired, perhaps, the invention of particle glass. To see light but not its source, to see something move outside but to be, at the same time, not quite sure of its form invites uncertainty into the house. Pinning a magnolia in our hair we wear our halter dress to the pool, soften into chlorinated water.

To lay claim to the world while, at the same, desiring the field overgrown by roses instead of the garden's fantastic topiary, the roadside graveyard instead of the military cemetery, headstones uniform. This I learned last summer alone in some other woman's country. A granite odalisque, she basks before shopping mall and Communist-era housing blocks.

# CELESTIAL SPHERE III

I wanted to love having sex with you in the grove, but the story kept intruding. With his fondness for the landscapes of Turner and Monet, the schoolboy, believing his teachers and his books, looks at the sea with an eye trained for linear and atmospheric perspective. By which I mean I could climax, sure, but remained nevertheless enclosed in a Pre-Raphaelite dress, magnolia crushed in my hair, I was held fast to the primordial experience of being hunted by large predators, a condition ritualized in sacrifice and war. I'm searching for details that create the intimacy of the spoken word, not details that enslave us to concepts.

But what approach to figuration initiates a more optimal mode of being? Little grains of saffron, ground cardamom, ginger scrapings in agreement with Bataille's conviction that sacrifice is the most profound, if ultimately futile, attempt by which humans try to re-establish intimacy with nature. Visiting the city I clutch my jacket close while longing to stand mind-blank and alone before artwork half-sculpture, half-painting. My body becomes real when we fur and bite, little drops of blood then sepia wash, bleached-out fields of white until all that's left is the sound of a bird and then weather.

To emerge from the corner as a form of persuasion, doubt released by a sentence contoured between Earth and moon. What is possible in sex: sacrificing our human aspect to the gods, we dissolve into salt moans of animality. Upon re-entering the day certainty falls short, for such experience destroys the idea of a tree as independent proposition, but rather proposition as a weaving into other propositions producing a compelling ground for a dark bed of pine and mulch so soft under shattering sensations of clarity.

But instead of dissolution, culture instructs a motif of Eros with accompanying blindfold, lamp, burning oil. If we believe Apuleius, Psyche will fare worse than Eve ever will: the Psyche-soul will be cast out, whipped by Worry and Sadness. Venus, omnipresent as both Morning Star and Evening Star, will bash Psyche's head into the ground, demand she labor to regain her place by sorting through piles of grain, fetch gold wool from violent sheep. *Go now*, she will command with a gesture of her long cold hand: fill a crystal ewer with dragon water, descend to the underworld to steal a dose of Proserpina's beauty, bring it back quickly in this little gilt box.

## CELESTIAL SPHERE IV

There were so many things the body wanted to say, but was it a change in climate or lack of cultivation that left us comparing our still life with the garden described in the book? Hum of power lines, a sensation of lawn soft underfoot. Or, you suggest, we might try ikebana, a three-branch asymmetrical attempt to arrange flowers as flowers. This differs from the image before me: a bouquet made of animal skin and organs.

I wasn't prepared for desire to feel like canvas stitched together, not in the manner of sails but of a balloon. And tethered at its mooring. Which didn't articulate the heart laid bare, gates thrown open, siege-engines on fire inside. Which made it nearly impossible to emerge with a display of neatly arranged piles of grain; gold wool not merely gathered but carded and spun; ewer filled to the top with violet water; little box heavy with pearls.

It seemed merely realistic to believe the balloon would expand, the ribcage having no other option but to crack admitting culture, tradition, history. This left me misty, a sense-impression of calla lilies, both white and yellow apprehended at a human, rather than a sky-like scale. What does it actually feel like to be Psyche illuminating her lover's body? My need for visual knowledge was fed by my sisters' speculations of aberration and monstrosity. But the transfer of weight, bending to his warmth: that was mine. And then the lamp tipped. And then the stench of sulfur.

Because I always believed inner nature to be subterranean, riverine, imagine my surprise when preoccupations fell, scales from eyes, and we were catching everything we touched on fire. Observation and instruction tell us cars don't grow out of earth, regardless of the field of abandoned Chevys photographed rusting into the desert. But note the revelation created by standing in the silence of the once burnt while, at the self-same time, being engulfed by one's own burning.

Alternately, one might try ikebana. Not that this would quiet the fire, cut free the balloon, but perhaps flower as flower would illuminate the stunning difference between exterior calm and the interior, which one never quite knows. Very little explanation exists as to why one should offer butchered animals to the deity for it is within the act, and only within the act, that the reason becomes self-evident. Happening upon a perfect star made by plastic chairs overturned by courtyard wind leads us to propose a great building containing all that might exist. Skepticism of this fact is akin to doubting the sacred before stepping off of a crowded Bucharest street into an Eastern Orthodox church. I admit to having been, at first, merely curious, the exterior reminding me of driving by the onion-domed churches of Ukrainian immigrants blooming up from Pennsylvania's mountain-top removal coal towns. Reminding me, that is to say, of home as a series of places I have never been. But upon entering, inhaling and exhaling incense and glittering icons I saw that like deep-sea bioluminescent creatures we might manufacture our own celestial light.

# CELESTIAL SPHERE V

Because I could still feel the small hardness in your voice, which I wanted to have been at least a large hardness, an American-sized granite canyon unsurpassable but magnificent. Instead, a recognition that we both had come to feel like a day unfolding as acid applied to velvet burning fabric to look like lace. Or perhaps when I said "Transcend into play" I said it with a little hurt mouth because transcendence must provide a bit of pain as when blood feathers are crushed by a well-meaning hand, a toy placed inconveniently in a cage.

Each morning proves a hypothesis: the world lists slightly more toward being than nonbeing. The season has started to shift although we've woken to our windows frozen over again. *But this is to be expected* reports the interlocutor in my ear, the foundation of a photograph indistinguishable from its referent, a relation not unlike that of a branded hide to its orange-red cattle brand. I've been standing on stage in my Psyche dress and shawl, face made up like an English rose reciting the philosophers' great schism. On the one hand those following Kant look for the attachment language makes with the world. They become an infant's mouth on a mother's breast. The others follow Hegel down an Eastern European street past dilapidated modernist buildings graffitied with Cyrillic admonitions, advertisements for fruit, for gas, a presidential candidate. I tell you this not to ignite a flame in your breast but rather to stand on stage singing birdcalls and folk motifs, an offering to the gods of public language.

To stand as if naked while others politely compliment my dove-gray dress, feathers dangling from my ears as I recount what it was like to be diverted into the little grove of elm. It was as if I didn't have a say in the matter, as if when I was walking home I didn't think to myself *Now be careful Psyche, you're leaving the path now, leaving your sisters behind now, now I am diverting into this little gloomy yet so romantic grove.* As if I hadn't watched myself walking there, embroidered shawl and slim leather sandals. *Tsk-tsk* says the mother in my head: *never return Tupperware empty and you are already late for work.* I didn't close the door politely, but with a culmination of I-statements, frost shaken off windows, for without sacrifice the world threatens to come undone.

To recount the shimmer of trout, rotted river grass, and a knife-gash releasing plastic beads from the fish's gut as the trees and the animals bow down. Winter births a season for being interior, underground, yes, but also hearth fire flickering *I will do my best by you* which sometimes means you the immigrant who doesn't yet speak English and sometimes you who turn to face the policeman with his dick-like club and his dick-like gun and sometimes you the philosopher in a cul-de-sac languishing and sometimes you the rose, your once-potent garden in weeds because who has time and everyone, we must admit, is slowly dying. But some mornings, for no given reason, the hypothesis appears delicate, deliberate, imagines Earth came into being all at once, foggy and blue and complete in its rush toward outer space while simultaneously being held back by the expanding embrace of the sun.

## COSMOGONY

               in answer to absence:
gutting the animal of what makes it
so beautiful

               remainder left to the field
carrion to crow     bones to mineral
fertilize a document

instruct     how to cross threshold
field     into home

                              each step taking
place into body until the body becomes
what songs     you claim     as your own

transfiguring space
                              between two things

nub of galena     tuning coil combine
for a little crystal radio     glitter-snow

transmitting    a true husk led me
to dwell
        to fall through firmament


become sky-dart    sky-cross    sky-
child reduced to ash    slurried over
the field to painted clouds


        bottom of backdrops
hoisted to the loft
        the sky-

flower's cycle of pale blue followed
by yellow berries animals eat
shat out    thus to grow
        a book
not possible    for its author to read

yet its red thread sews the skull's
temple    as time sews
temple    to sacred space

                              to the sea       and
taking the boat out     letting it drift
lifting up one's drowsy head and then
letting it     again drift
                              the mind filling

each glass globe with oil       antifreeze
glycerin     allows the
                              glitter to float
nomad     maenad     small inclination
toward being

whistling in power lines     artifact
fragments of sky gods lost
long ago

                              to be this against what     of yourself
                              you decided to keep: star chart     little
                              model boat     to find

                                          your voice     grooved
                              vinyl     had been music

# NOTES

"I was looking at the flower bed by the front door; 'That is the whole,' I said. I was looking at a plant with a spread of leaves; and it seemed suddenly plain that the flower itself was a part of the earth; that a ring enclosed what was the flower; and that was the real flower; part earth; part flower."

– Virginia Woolf, "A Sketch of the Past"

# GEOSPHERE I

*...Fort! Da!—though we both know the bus station's too far to reach by foot...*

In the famous second section of his 1920 book *Beyond the Pleasure Principle* Sigmund Freud turns from the "dark and dismal subject of the traumatic neurosis" he had been addressing—railway crashes and shrapnel, disasters of technology and the First World War—to examine the psyche at work in "normal" activities: in children's play. Freud's objects of study are the games of little Ernst, the son of his beloved second daughter, Sophie. In this text Freud refers to Sophie not as "Sophie" or as "my daughter" but as "the child's mother," refers to Ernst not by name or as "grandson" but as "the child," thus reinforcing the signature objective tone of modern foundation myths.

The child's game involves a simple toy, a little "wooden reel with a piece of string tied around it...what the child did was to hold the reel by the string and very skillfully throw it over the edge of the child's curtained cot, so that it disappeared into it." Upon the disappearance of the object the child would utter "o-o-o," thought by Freud and "the mother" to be baby talk for *Fort!* (German for "gone"), and accompanied by "an expression of interest and satisfaction." When the child reels the object back into view the child utters a joyous sound approximating *Da!* (German for "there"). Freud notes but does not take up the idea that "As a rule one only witnessed [the] first act, which was repeated untiringly as a game in itself, though there is no doubt that the greater pleasure was attached to the second act." Yes, no doubt.

Freud reads the child's action of "staging the disappearance and return of objects within the child's reach" as "compensating" for allowing the mother to go away without protesting—for suppressing the broadcasting capacity of the body, the physical grasping-after that the intimate other's disappearance evokes. When wondering how the act of departure, in particular, operates within the pleasure principle Freud notes that when the mother leaves the child falls into a passive, overpowered position. When repeating the disappearance in the game, however, the child takes on an active role. This is not only an instinct for mastery, Freud asserts, but of revenge and defiance, the child later developing the habit of sending toys with which the child was angry "To the fwont!" that is to say, to war.

With this comment we notice Freud's return to the subject of war and death despite himself. Ashes, ashes, we all fall down. This inevitability crescendos in section five of the essay when Freud posits the "death instinct" as primary over all other drives, for "the goal of all life is death." Even drives that we consider "life-preserving" function only to protect life so that we can die "in our own way," which we might assume to mean by natural causes rather than by trauma of accident or war. Do we see proof or contradiction in Freud's own life? He was to deny the danger he was in as a Jew, not leaving Austria until Hitler's invasion in 1938 even though in 1933 his books had been publically burned in Berlin. Four of his five sisters would die in concentration camps as the 82 year-old Freud, ravaged by cancer, was driven into exile. He was to die within the year, assisted by his doctor into death with a heavy dose of morphine.

Children's games—and acts of imagination—transform what is unpleasurable into an entity that, instead of exceeding the self (as all that is unpleasurable is wont to do), becomes a mental object that can be recollected and worked over. An object of pleasure even if akin to the pleasure of worrying a loose tooth, the pain it evokes reminding the self that the mouth is alive.

An act of imagination, the essay, as form, provides a theater of actions over which its writer has considerable, yet nevertheless limited, agency. Is this incompletion an instance of fidelity mimetic of the real? *Beyond the Pleasure Principle* was published the year Sophie died of the post-war influenza epidemic and includes the note, "When the child was five years and nine months old, his mother died. Now that she was really 'gone' ('o-o-o'), the boy showed no grief over her. Indeed, a second child had been born in the meantime and had awakened in him the strongest jealousy." Did Freud's objective use of "the child" rather than "my grandson Ernst," of "the child's mother" rather than "my daughter Sophie" save his teeth from aching, protect his skull from splitting as he skimmed through the published volume of his text, alighting on the domestic scenario he had recorded in his description of the game? Alighting upon his own conviction that no doubt the return of the lost object—of the little wooden reel, of the mother, of his daughter—would be, although impossible, the greatest pleasure?

## GEOSPHERE III

*...I'm entranced by your period of sitting before still lifes, oysters shucked and exuding.... Venus appearing at first to be caught coursing backwards through sky...*

The pearl oyster contains a treasure, a planet, a pearl. The edible oyster contains a delicacy, an aphrodisiac, a sensation of eating the ocean, sex cradled primal in the mouth. Hesiod writing his cosmology in 700 BC associates the origins of Aphrodite with the oyster in a time before Zeus when the first god, the sky god, is castrated by Cronos his Titan son. Cronos flings the sky god's testicles into the sea and from this foam Aphrodite is born. From *aphros*, aphrodisiac, erotic origin, symbol of fertility, pleasure, sex rising upon an oyster shell, Eros her constant companion. The Romans translate Aphrodite into Venus, the maternal-imperial, and Julius Caesar claims descent as she comes to symbolize Roman power, sexual allure, and martial dominance. And in this time Eros becomes Cupid, often portrayed as Venus's child, pleasure shifting from mother to son with the precision of an arrow arced from an exacting bow.

Roman astronomers named the planet Venus in our sky. Similar in structure and size to Earth, Venus spins in the opposite direction without moons or rings, thick atmosphere trapping heat. Volcanic, this planet's greenhouse effect renders surface temperatures hot enough to melt lead. In naming the planet Romans couldn't have realized these traits, would not have known how acutely they illustrate the condition of desire. They understood only the planet's distant brightness—diamond, utterance, pearl—

not her swampy heat or that she spins nearly upright and therefore doesn't experience seasons, just as (love-sick, and consumed with thoughts of the beloved) one might walk barefoot over frost-ridden grass. Interior metal melted, molten, language fused to weather system.

In visual art the oyster remains a symbol of Aphrodite and Venus through antiquity, the Middle Ages, the Renaissance, and the Baroque. As Liana De Girolami Cheney discusses in her article "The Oyster in Dutch Genre Paintings: Moral or Erotic Symbolism," Renaissance paintings taking up the popular "feasts of the gods" theme depict oysters in scenes when Venus, reclining almost always nude and sometimes wearing pearls, makes merry with other gods and mortals at a banquet in a grove. Dutch early-Baroque paintings, 1610-1630, take up this same theme but instead of cavorting gods and goddesses we find affluent mortals well-dressed and dining in rooms fitted out with spoils of colonization: gilded leather wallpaper, Turkish carpets, silver ewers, heavy goblets, plates piled with meats and fruits and oysters—always abundant oysters. According to Cheney, from 1630-1660 the oyster disappears from feast scenes but then reappears, made popular again by the 1658 Dutch domination of pearl fisheries in Indian waters. Among these later paintings emerges a new genre of intimate interiors: two or three people share a plate of oysters, exchange knowing glances in lamplight glimmering a dark room. During its 1630-1660 hiatus from feast tableaux the oyster persists as a central feature in Dutch still-life paintings, a genre that began and flourished in the Netherlands at the beginning of the seventeenth century, popular in the new state of abundance created by the rise of industrialization and colonization. These "advances" gave humans the power to regulate plenty and lack, and to separate resources from the land and traditions that had held them. Oyster shucked and then pearl. Oyster sucked and swallowed.

My first encounter with the exceptional Dutch still-life tables featuring oysters had been a grainy reproduction in Norman Bryson's *Looking at the Overlooked: Four Essays on Still Life Paintings*. While each oyster painting is unique, in canvas after canvas Willem Claesz Heda and Pieter Claesz, both masters of the form, evoke harmony in the perfect framing of the table, in the symmetry of ewer and goblet, in the repetition of oval shapes: oyster, lemon, pewter plate, and glass. The graceful helix of a peeled rind, tobacco falling from paper twists. Most of Heda's and Claesz's tables are depicted after the feast has been eaten or as if the diner, always singular, has just stepped away, goblets in disarray. Yet, even so this harmony appears effortless, as if a byproduct of consumption.

Or perhaps there is a harmony in objects that persists despite humanity's chaotic disruption? "In a certain sense," Bryson writes, "the harmony requires a certain degree of *forcing*, and this is very clear in Claesz's use of 'monochrome' technique…. Claesz deliberately evens out tonality and expands the middle range of greys, while at the same time filtering all colors through a distinctive brown-green. The natural tones and colors of the objects are keyed to the translucent bottle green of a glass beaker or *roemer*."

Intrigued by Bryson's description of the painting (objects keyed to translucent bottle green) and of his concept of "forced harmony" dependent not only on arrangement but on color, I Google Heda's and Claesz's oyster paintings (*Still Life with Wine Glass and Silver Bowl; Still Life with Oysters; Still Life with Turkey Pie*, etcetera) and am immediately overtaken by their mood. The solitary scene, the gleam of light off silver. In one painting a wine glass is tipped, shattered. In another the oyster plate precariously balances on the edge of the table. In all of the paintings the oysters glow as if internally illuminated leaving a taste of silver in my mouth, a taste like stepping from a quiet Bucharest street, blue-light snow, into the metallic shimmer of an Orthodox church.

Intoxicated by this taste but far from Bucharest, I visit the Met's gallery 635 where Heda's *Still Life with Oysters, a Silver Tazza, and Glassware* hangs next to Claesz's *Still Life with a Skull and Writing Quill.* Claesz's painting has the weight of earth while Heda's oysters pulse through a darkened room with white lead light, a luminosity picked up by the window reflected in the curved surface of the glass *roemer,* prunts on the stem to steady a greasy-fingered drinker's grip on the glass at a time when forks were not commonly used. And the white illumination of the oysters echoes out in stippling along the edge of the silver tazza, beading the glass ewer ghosting at the back.

Still-life painting complicates the long-standing question of what the image should do. Should it strike us viscerally (see the oyster in the painting and your mouth waters. See the curve of a shoulder in lamplight and your shoulder then softens, a beautiful back revealed and your back burns and the heavy knife in Cronos's hand becomes a heavy weight in your own)? And so you become seeing, move into the interior of images as the images move into you. Or should the still life challenge the mind, engage the viewer in a self-consciously symbolic system, a discourse of pattern? The poem says *oyster in my mouth, pearl in my belly, gleaming lamp in my hand.* The essay says *sign* and *sign* and *sign.* What emerges between says *yes* and *more* and *both* as she licks salt off her lips, eyes wet with so much looking.

# HYDROSPHERE III

*…As an ode to the Law of Similarity and the Law of Contact…*

Michael Taussig's *Mimesis and Alterity* proposes a sensate form of knowing engrossed in its object, an "active yielding and mirroring of the knower in the unknown, of thought in its objects." Taussig asserts that this claim for activity challenges the predominate critique of mimesis as negative passivity, Theodor Adorno and Max Horkheimer for example in the *Dialectic of Enlightenment* connect mimesis with the "trend to lose oneself in the environment…the tendency to let oneself go and sink back into nature." This passive falling is connected with Freud's death instinct, and Adorno and Horkheimer assert that the elimination of such surrender is crucial to any form of cultural development.

The tension between active and passive imitation—between regarding mimesis as favorable or unfavorable—goes back to Platonic and Aristotelian roots. Initially the term only referred to acts of performance (mime, dance, and music) aimed at representing inner reality. Jocasta's broaches of beaten gold, their long pins, the softness of Oedipus's eyes. A semantic shift in the fifth century BC applied the concept to imitations of the external world, thus giving the term a dual orientation. Plato and Aristotle use both senses, but most often address mimesis as representation of the internal. This dual valance and the question of the difference between representation and imitation come to reverberate through ethical and aesthetic judgments of art.

In his exploration of mimesis as active yielding Taussig turns to indigenous knowledge and "sympathetic magic," elaborating upon the Law of Similarity and the Law of Contact, the two great principles delineated by George Frazer in *The Golden Bough*. In the Law of Similarity like begets like, an effect resembles its cause, and therefore a magician or shaman can produce any desired effect by imitating it: pierce an effigy with a needle and the person it is modeled on will suffer in this same spot. In such systems the extent to which the copy visually resembles the original doesn't appear to influence the efficacy of the magic—but what the copy has been made of matters. For example, Frazer notes that Peruvian Indians in 1621 were discovered to burn images of persons hated or feared and if the image was to represent an Indian it was made of llama fat mixed with corn; if a Spaniard, pig fat and wheat, materials associated with colonizing power. In contrast, the Law of Contact assumes things once in contact with each other continue to act on each other at a distance—even after physical connection has been severed. Thus we get love spells and death charms involving hair, nails, semen, excrement, footprints, and teeth.

Mirror neurons, identified in the 1990s, show that we are always internally mimicking and might be read as the interior's instantiation of the Laws of Similarity and Contact. Cells in our brains activate when we perform certain actions—and when we observe others performing the same action. When I see you smile, the familiar example goes, I smile not as a conscious response or because I find myself to be happy, but because my mirror neurons have fired, creating neural activity that we associate with the act of smiling, a collapse between seeing and doing that throws into question what exactly it means "to be happy." Alternatively, who hasn't felt the need to cry when seeing tears, to vomit when another vomits, to wince with pain as another is hit?

Furthermore, might not the application to mirror neurons of the Laws of Similarity and Contact imply we are all made of the same material? What other explanation accounts for the fact that when you are pierced and wince with pain I, seeing you wince, without thinking wince back? In larger gestures of the body we can also see the dual internal-external articulation of mimesis. The reason we attribute emotion to a performing dancer or actress is because we experience our own emotions with similar, albeit less stylized, gestures. And so we see in our own felt expressions of joy, hatred, pleasure, and pain the original sense of mimesis as external representation of inner states.

At the same time we well might wonder the extent to which our physical gestures are modeled on external cultural constructions, learned long before we knew what we were learning. My smile is perhaps not technically my smile at all, but rather is just a good imitation of my mother's smile, which is, in turn, a good imitation of her mother's smile and the act of smiling as practiced by our culture. On one hand this suggests a horror-film scenario of a hall of mirrors echoing smile after smile after smile, unattached to any feeling human. On the other hand, might there not be something intriguing in the idea that one's smile—as well as one's trauma—is never one's own, but rather a palimpsest of ancestral gestures, a portable cultural heirloom?

# HYDROSPHERE V

*...our kneeling on the riverbank next to dead crayfish and we cried there, rubbing mud into arms and chests...*

From 1973-1980 Cuban-born artist Ana Mendieta performs the over one hundred site-specific works of her *Silueta (Silhouette)* series in natural environments of Iowa and Mexico. A merger of painting, sculpture, and performance, Mendieta uses her naked body as instrument, imprints a figure in the earth, or builds a female form out of dirt, flowers, tree branches, moss, gunpowder, and fire, occasionally combined with animal hearts or handprints branded into the ground. She most often performs alone and without an audience, her ephemeral traces left to erode with the elements, documented only by film and photographs. For example the film *Untitled (Genesis Buried in Mud)* shows a rocky patch of land, and the viewer slowly realizes her naked body breathes beneath the mud. Or in her three-minute-ten-second Super-8 *Corazón de roca con sangre* (*Rock Heart with Blood*) we see her kneel in the nude near a woman-shaped impression in the earth, paint a heart-shaped rock with blood, and set it there. Filling the imprint with red pigment, she then places her body facedown in the shape.

These imprints with their lack of detail don't read as self-portraits but as active and intentional forms gesturing to a larger cosmology. As art historian Susan Best notes, arms overhead depict a merger of earth and sky or floating in water, actualizing the space between land and sea. Or arms raised and legs held together signify a wandering soul. Concerned not only with the shape she makes, but also with the materials she engages, Mendieta contrasts her work with contemporaneous land-art practitioners who have often displayed a Western, phallocentric domination over nature: "My work is basically in the tradition of a Neolithic artist. It has very little to do with most earth art. I'm not interested in the formal qualities of my material, but their emotional and sensual ones," Mendieta writes of her process, referring to the earth as "maternal" and her practice as distinctly feminine, seeking to resuscitate a link between the female body and space.

If gender and self are performative mimetic constructions (Judith Butler's "stylized repetition of acts") the type of self, the type of gender Mendieta constructs with her *Silueta* series offers an alternative in stark contrast to contemporary performances of self so engrossed in the spectacle, audience, and commodity ubiquitous in social-media culture. Each of the one hundred-plus *Siluetas* requires repetitive gesture, but also is individually unique, improvised. And, while the *Siluetas* engage cultural forms of goddess imagery and concepts that stitch the feminine to the earth, instead of narrowing identity into these essentializing forms, the *Siluetas* use these forms to let the body seep beyond its physical and symbolic boundary, emphasizing gesture over object, material over image, ephemerality over fixity, plurality over monolith.

Here we find an active yielding that echoes the boundary-effacing "magic" of the Laws of Similarity and Contact replete with what Taussig calls the power of "breaking away from the tyranny of the visual notion of image," as in the example of "Navaho sand-painting…said to cure not by the patients' looking at the pictures inscribed therein, but by their placing their body in the design itself." In grass, in sand and dirt, set on fire and filmed or photographed then left to wash away. This affordance of gesture, as Carrie Noland suggests in *Agency and Embodiment*, gives the body "a chance to feel itself moving through space," creating the opportunity to challenge the cultural scripts we necessarily always already embody.

Mendieta's 1972 series *Glass on Body Imprints* also thrives on repetitive action and female image-making, but eschews all the senses of beauty so prominent in the *Silueta* series. During the performance Mendieta stands facing the viewer/camera, presses a large square of plexiglass against her face, then against her breasts, back, torso, pubis, and buttocks. Thirty-six color slides, 13 of which she had printed in black and white, document the performance. Tightly framed, they crop out all but the area being pressed. The images show these body parts as flattened, squashed, deformed, and mutated. While the viewer is aware that she is only seeing a temporary distortion of the female body, the effect is of disfiguring violence: the figure's breasts are twisted; the edge of the plexiglass square digs into her stomach; her face contorted, grotesque, as in a slow-motion punch, lips enlarged, eyes folded under flesh as the image hardens into headshot-sized photographs. As with the *Siluetas*, in this project Mendieta also presses her naked body into the world. But whereas the *Siluetas* create a connective, positively valued series of gestures, this piece speaks to the repeated violence of disconnection, separation, and individuation entailed by objectification and abuse.

These images produce an affective response of pain—viewing the photographs I automatically wince. At the same time the materials Mendieta uses intrigue. This includes her body, yes, but also that square of plexiglass, a transparent and human-made substance that causes disconnection and doesn't allow the self to transcend its boundaries. Here I think of transparent but powerful forces: the gaze that imprints its object with judgment and presupposition; the shift between seeing and staring; law, which contains, divides, constricts. The body presses against a substance that unlike the earth resists its trace.

As with the *Silueta* series, while the *Glass on Body Imprints* impact emotionally they are impersonal: one has the feeling that Mendieta means us to realize that any woman might stand in the place of the woman in the photographs, although her dark hair and Cuban features also ask us to think of the female immigrant body often so invisibly visible in the world as housekeeper, maid, nanny.

If we are familiar with the artist's biography, the *Glass on Body Imprints* will perhaps suggest that mimesis might not only imitate the past, supplying presence in the space of absence, but might also be, itself, imitated by subsequent events. This series reads forward to her mysterious and violent death in 1985. Thirteen years after creating the photographs she will fall from the 34th-floor window of the apartment she shares with her husband, Carl Andre, and will die on impact with the roof of the bodega below. While Andre, charged with murder, who has scratches on his nose and arms, will tell variable stories about the event—and a doorman will testify to having heard fighting, a woman's voice screaming "No-no-no" right before the sound of Mendieta hitting the bodega roof—he will be acquitted for lack of evidence.

And backwards: in *Impossible Returns: Narratives of the Cuban Diaspora* Iraida H. López begins her chapter on Mendieta with a scene from September of 1961. After the Bay of Pigs, Mendieta, 12 years old, and her older sister wait in *la pecera*, the glass-enclosed space known as "the fishbowl" inside the Havana airport. They are participants in Operation Peter Pan, an effort run by the United States to transport children from Castro's Cuba. She and her sister will be relocated to Iowa, living first in a refugee camp and then in a series of foster homes. In *Los que se fueron* (*Those Who Left*), Estela Bravo's 1980 documentary about the tens of thousands of children who left Cuba for the United States without their parents, Mendieta remembers this moment as "having been torn from my homeland," her mother and father on the other side of the glass putting their hands to the fishbowl, trying to connect.

# BIOSPHERE I

*…structures calling to mind Lee Bontecou's canvas-stretched steel constructions…*

Before encountering Lee Bontecou's work I dreamed a shipwreck, translucent bottle green, and one of her constructions washed up on shore. In the dream I woke next to canvas and steel covered in seaweed, and as I dried in the sun the structure's planes and curves turned to gold and shadow. This translated into writing, my main character—my I—inhabiting the sculpture as shelter from the elements. Into the black hole at the center I'd climb and the wind would cease as my body warmed, became velvet granuled with sand. The story documenting this dream, phrases of which I can still see before me, is long lost. Sometimes I try to find it, search through old thumb drives and disks. I'm both skeptical and certain this writing exists, that I knew Bontecou's structures before witnessing them, recognition supplementing the raw experience of encounter.

While I'd like to think this recognition signals something special about me, my kinship with Bontecou, it is more likely that Bontecou's artwork taps into something primal, something exceeding all of us and known before birth. As Donald Judd suggests in his 1965 essay much of her work's power comes from a rare engagement with the image: "Usually an image is a form which primarily suggests something else," but the black hole center of a Bontecou structure "is not primarily allusive and descriptive. The black hole does not allude to a black hole; it is one." And perhaps, further, there is something elemental drawn out by her use of canvas, a material harvested from fibers that grow as protection of the cotton seed. And this protection she then stretches over steel frames smelted from iron ore, the last element created so long ago via a supernova's fusion just before its collapse scatters iron into space and thus into the still-forming Earth.

Known in dream, in museum, her structures returned to me in Bucharest in the form of the city's modernist buildings, concrete and pollution-blackened, and yet a ticking internal elegance in the rounded corner of Marcel Iancu's 1930s building at number three Stefan Luchian strada, or in the angles of his Solly Gold apartment building, its blunt suggestion of the industrial, of the utilitarian. And yet the courtyard's huntress bas-relief, delicate, harmonizes even as it contrasts. I lingered at the wrought iron gate as the lace curtains in surrounding windows trembled with the breath of watchers. Never before had I been on an urban street so swollen with silence that sound shattered, reminding me of a new model of the Earth that hypothesizes our core was formed by first a slow percolation of iron and then searing from the mantel to interior.

Industrial materials drawn together with a sense of the hand, stitched here, tied with wire here, lined with velvet here, coated with soot. Never before had the conversation between velvet and soot been so intimate and never before had what dominates, stands through time, been so overtly fragile. As Elyse Speaks observes in "The Terms of Craft and Other Means of Making," Bontecou, her studio, its welding torch and sewing machine create hybrid forms that are at once paintings mounted on the wall and sculptures hovering, skeletons of buildings and boats, sails and tents. Carapaces, shells, exposed membranes. Two utterances harnessed in a dialogue. From the belly of her structure I spoke the languages of sand.

As with all love, it is not only that I choose again and again these artworks: they also again and again choose me. I recognize them and am recognized by them, constituted. A passage that lingers with me, describing this phenomenon, opens the philosopher Alenka Zupančič's essay "The Case of the Perforated Sheet:"

> Lacan depicts what he calls the "metaphor of love" with this poignant image: a hand reaches out toward a fruit, a flower, or lips which suddenly blaze; its attempt to attain, to draw near, to make the fire burn, is closely connected with the ripening of the fruit, the beauty of the flower, the blazing of the lips. But when, in this attempt to attain, to draw near, to make the fire burn, the hand has moved far enough toward the object, another hand springs up from the fruit, from the flower, from the lips, and reaches out to meet our hand, and at this moment our hand freezes in the closed fullness of the fruit, in the open fullness of the flower, in the explosion of the blazing hand. That which occurs at this moment is love.

The experience of "to choose" becomes different from standing before a vitrine saying "I would like to have *this* and *this* and *this*. Or nothing here is good enough for me." It cascades, a process of interaction, a gesture *toward*, which is always entwined with its substance even before one can know if the other will gaze back. Steel and copper, dominance of browns, tans, blacks, a persistent sense that her materials have industrial pasts. "Vagina dentate," says one critic. "Feminine black hole mystery," says another.

In Central and Eastern European cities, perched between two world wars, modernism sprang forth in the form of machines to live in, and this living was to have unfolded a utopia so closely connected with the ripening of fruit. Was to have unfolded. Could have unfolded, little paper flowers which upon touching water open. When history is done with us we are left with the luminescence of materials touched and again touched and worn through. "What else to do if the object you look at suddenly looks back at you, thus producing an undeniable effect of subjectivation?" Zupančič writes. "You either run away or fall, that is, resubjectivize accordingly." Resubjectivized, the forms blaze.

# BIOSPHERE III

*…its story is discovered written on papyrus strips used for Egyptian mummification…*

Many of the papier-mâché mummy cases of Hellenistic Egypt were constructed of papyrus scraps discarded by scribes at Alexandria when they made errors while copying manuscripts. Discovered during the great excavations at the turn of the century, it was not until the 1960s that technology was advanced enough to separate and read the fragile fragments without effacing the text. A key find in 1965 was part of the *Erechtheus*, a lost play composed by Euripides during the Golden Age of Greece: a copy of the manuscript had been cut into the shape of wings to create a Horus falcon ornamenting a mummy case. Only 125 lines of the play had been known prior to this discovery when 250 additional lines spoken by Athena near the end of the play were carefully extracted, preserved, recognized, and translated.

It would take 40 more years before archaeologist Joan Breton Connelly was to connect the events of the play with the Parthenon frieze finding that the architectural panel long thought to depict a golden robe offered to Athena actually pictures a funerary dress. And the female figure in the panel is no mere acolyte, but rather is the sacrificial heroine herself, shown in the act of helping to unfold her last garment. This new insight, Connelly argues in *The Parthenon Enigma*, her 2014 book on the discovery, asks us to reevaluate not only the symbolic system of the Parthenon, but also the very foundations of Western democratic values formed during the Golden Age of Greece when Perikles, ruler of Athens, rebuilt the Acropolis from the rubble of the recent Persian Wars. Long a sacred site focused around the Old Athena Temple and the Old Parthenon, the Acropolis had housed among other things a snake that ceased eating its honey cakes, thus warning Athens of the coming Persian invasion. But Perikles does not merely reconstruct what had stood before. Instead, in 447 BC he begins to build new temples out of freshly quarried Greek marble from the city's own Mount Pentelikon. The structures honor Athena, and Perikles adds a temple to Erechtheus, both progenitors of Athens and vessels of Grecian value.

The figure of Erechtheus celebrated by classical Greece merges a prehistoric sixth king of Athens, who reigned in Mycenae during the fourteenth century BC at the time the first palace was built atop the Acropolis, with a mythological character born when the blacksmith god Hephaestus, chasing Athena in lust, spilled his seed upon her leg. Disgusted, Athena wipes his semen from her thigh with a piece of cloth she throws on the ground, thus impregnating the earth. Erechtheus, born of Gaia, is raised by Athena in her temple atop the Acropolis. When he grows he marries Praxithea, a nymph born of the great river Kephisos, thus uniting the children of earth and water. The plot thickens when Athens is threatened by Poseidon's son and Erechtheus asks the oracle at Delphi what he should do to protect the city. The oracle announces that he must sacrifice his youngest daughter. When Erechtheus asks Praxithea to consent to this sacrifice she immediately makes a rousing political speech proudly offering her daughter without hesitation.

We have long known this speech, preserved as part of a trial oration made by the Athenian Lykourgos. Athens, Praxithea reasons, warrants saving at any cost, for it is autochthonic: made not of a people brought from elsewhere but of those born of its own land. This is the heart of its greatness, she says, and the reason Athenians have children is to protect the altars of the land's gods. She reminds Erechtheus that they would quickly send a son to war and so a daughter, in this spirit, should be sent to sacrifice. Furthermore, how could she be so selfish as to save her daughter and condemn her husband, her three other daughters, and her fellow citizens to death? What is the life of one in the face of the destruction of this city, of so many?

The youngest daughter, known only as "Parthenos" or "maiden," is sacrificed and Athens is saved. Praxithea, however, must suffer other losses. Erechtheus is swallowed by an earthquake caused by Poseidon, and her three remaining daughters, who had made a secret suicide pact with their younger sister, leap off the steep edge of the Acropolis.

The lost lines of Euripides's play find Praxithea alone in the middle of the Acropolis. Athena comes to her there and makes a speech, a divine command for the construction of the two great temples of the Sacred Rock: the Parthenon and the Erechtheion. Praxithea must bury her husband in one spot, erecting the temple over him. Carapace, shell, the languages of sand. Her daughters Athena will send to the heavens as stars to be known as the Hyacinth goddesses, and their bodies Praxithea must bury in a single tomb, a practice usually reserved for warriors. The youngest is to be honored for her sacrifice, the elder daughters for their loyalty. Above them the Parthenon must be built. Along with overseeing this construction, Athena appoints Praxithea as priestess, instructing her to tend both sacred temples: an honor celebrating her nobility, selflessness, and strength.

Connelly notes that Euripides's play was likely first performed around 422, just as both of the structures were being finished: "*Erechtheus* would have been presented in the Theater of Dionysus on the south slope of the Acropolis and the play would have been viewed by thousands," infusing the architectural site with mythological history. Here we might again think of the dual-valance of mimesis as representation of the internal and imitation of the external. Would Atheneans have recognized Praxithea to be an external symbol of the internal condition of being Athenean?

Of being human? Of being woman? Cochineal-dyed linen. And with Praxithea's speech does Euripides intend a companion example to Agamemnon's sacrifice of Iphigenia? The play doesn't give voice to the daughter, but the fact that on the Parthenon's panel she holds up her own funerary dress indicates that her mother was not the only person in her family who actively accepted the role of sacrifice. Or does Euripides intend an ironic judgment of the warrior whose success is predicated on the death of virgins? Regardless, Perikles's Acropolis and Euripides's *Erechtheon* make it clear that democracy requires—and makes sacred—pain and loss.

Connelly's careful reading of material objects, of papyrus and stone, not only details the story of her discovery, but also serves to excavate Perikles's Parthenon from 2500 years of history, showing the ways in which the structure has been physically and conceptually formed and reformed in an image not of its original intent—but of each age that seizes upon its symbolic power. Her prologue alone takes us through a breathtaking trajectory of conversion, appropriation, and interpretation. In 389 AD the Roman emperor will issue decrees banning temples, statues, festivals, and by the end of the sixth century the Parthenon will be transformed into a Christian church dedicated to the Virgin Mary. Crusaders in 1204 convert this Greek Orthodox cathedral into a Roman Catholic one. Ottoman Turks in 1458 conqueror Athens, rebuilding the Parthenon as a mosque. Enlightenment scholars narrate classical Greece in their own self-image, and in the early nineteenth century aristocrats will remove the Parthenon's marble sculptures to the British Museum where they remain despite vigorous debate, having been described by the collection's curator as late as the 1990s as "a pictorial representation of England as a free society and the liberator of other peoples." And consider the to-scale replica of the Parthenon in Nashville, Tennessee, continuing America's tradition of absorbing immigrant iconography—the structure built not of marble hewn from the city's source, but of concrete.

# ATMOSPHERE I

*…The question then: how to make a self, text, world outside established pattern but familiar enough to read?…*

Yayoi Kusama's immersive art installation *The Infinity Mirrored Room—The Souls of Millions of Light Years Away* (2013) is not much larger than a walk-in closet that has been mirror-lined, illuminated only by 75 multi-colored LED bulbs that flicker and pulse. And yet the space casts the viewer, who must enter the experience alone, into boundless sensation that's like looking down at Los Angeles at night from the roof deck of the Griffith Park Observatory and then looking at the Milky Way through the observatory's Zeiss telescope and then with naked eye looking at the city and then with the telescope at planets, stars, and dust. The experience Kusama creates is like this, except *The Infinity Mirrored Room's* heavens and city happen all at once, and as foreground and background collapse you not only feel as small as a point of light but you, transparent and shimmering, have multiplied. Unsphered the body becomes weightless, as if in space, in salt water floating, and the mind doesn't attach to any singular self-reflection above the infinity of others.

What if we conceive of subject-formation to be like this, exceeding Lacan's mirror phase, its famous moment when as infants we encounter our own image in a mirror, in another's gaze, recognizing in this image our ego-ideal, which had been always already waiting for us, a culturally constructed identity? By time we are absolved from remembering this first identification and each subsequent encounter comes upon us so rapidly, the process of recognition and refraction becomes the thing that I am. Puncturing this echo are moments when we see ourselves looking, wanting to identify but instead finding ourselves flickering between acts of looking and the multiple floating images we want, or are told we want, ourselves to be. *Little princess, bride, and mother,* culture said from my girlhood vanity with oval mirror, but I was already standing before the ballet-studio mirror visualizing exact forms no body ever perfectly imitates. *Ronde de jamb, ronde de jamb, ronde de jamb.*

We learn that the more precisely we mimic the ego-ideal the more legible we become to others and yet only between individual and ideal—between seeker and darling, between body and arabesque—does freedom, agency, and potentiality spark. This revelation comes to me again and again in the language of Emily Dickinson, Virginia Woolf, H.D., Hélène Cixous, Clarice Lispector, Mina Loy, their poems, essays, fictions flashing with *ostranenie* and dislocation igniting in the sternum and then radiating through arms and an uplift of the head. A lyric instruction for counteracting forces that pull multiplicity into unified image. For example, understanding the ego-ideal of feminine subjectivity to be predicated on existing as some man's love object, Mina Loy in 1914 writes that women must actively "destroy in themselves the desire to be loved…the feeling that it is a personal insult when a man transfers his attentions from her to another woman…they must destroy the desire for comfortable protection instead of an intelligent curiosity & courage in meeting & resisting the pressure of life." Loy's writing floods the mind, becomes a sensation of electrified power coursing under skin, tones of purple-black velvet streaked with garnet and ruby, a combination of softness and serration.

This softness and serration linger within and beyond language in daily tasks of walking the dog, doing the dishes, going to work, the thought of destruction-as-a-cause-for-coming-into-being not something grand and ideological, but instead activated by feeling into small gestures. There is self-making authorship in this—seedlings of agency available in any act, from the most mundane practice of settling into a chair to the focused movement of yogi, sufi, and dancer. Who would we be if we saw the ego-ideal not as a perfect image, but as a series of selves generating connective ideas, conduits for the nerve impulses of interconnection, our bodies through language and gesture exchanging information of felt sense with one another, with animate and inanimate environments?

To feel the body includes being supported in its position by the chair or reclined on the couch and cradled. Then standing to walk across the room, legs charged with the muscular energy of a tiger, the torso an electrical storm system, arms fluid, dahlia-headed. To feel this, bathed in blue because the window gives dusk and snow, a thickness of light, carpet lush beneath feet, this going on regardless of noticing. But when noticing, tendons and muscles tighten such that you inhabit this space, blue, part plush.

The word "problem" derives from late fourteenth-century Old French, which comes from the Latin *problema*, itself from the Greek: "a task, that which is proposed, a question," also "anything projecting, headland, promontory, fence, barrier"; a "thing put forward." A dahlia with its petal-packed complexity, although to be precise each petal is a floret, a flower of its own. I stood inside *The Infinity Mirrored Room* and found myself multiplied, reality exceeding the familiar. Akin to feather-packed flower heads, which are always a multiplicity or the result of artificial cultivation, for the most densely petaled flower in nature is the buttercup with its five yellow, green, or white petals sometimes flushed with purple, red, and pink.

But even this wildflower, thought so sweet and innocent blooming along the road, defies its simple image; it is in fact highly poisonous, causes the skin to blister and, if swallowed, internal burning and vomiting. Animals avoid the flower, intuiting this, while humans override instinct: children in a game press a buttercup to the tender skin below a playmate's chin. A red welt means you love butter. Taken into the mouth the flowers have an acrid taste.

What if instead of a mathematical puzzle with an answer, we considered a problem as a promontory, a headland, a landscape you've woken to realize might be approached in a number of ways, taking one's time up the side of the mountain inhaling sage, wild flowers, Manzanita-tangled switchbacks, and watching as night falls over Los Angeles, the edge between self and lights and stars diminishing?

Language, like the body in its organic and permeable flux, has as much potential to constitute a technology for traveling, subverting, depositing agentic seed as it does to embed cultural norms, instantiate a pre-given ego-ideal. This power cannot be separated from the life lived. As translator Leslie Anne Boldt writes in her introduction to Georges Bataille's *Inner Experience*: "We are babblers when we limit our use of language to utilitarian ends, when we make it serviceable to the projects through which we sidestep our anxiety. This abuse of language mirrors the abuse which we make of our existence: we have denatured it in removing from it the trace of the sacred, in our blind observance of the dictums of project and work."

# ATMOSPHERE II

*...performed mid-stage in blue, scooping red earth from a pail, running hands over thighs, hips, breasts...*

Pina Bausch's version of the *Rite of Spring*, choreographed in 1975, begins with the stage covered in peat, a spotlight illuminating a dancer in a fawn-colored slip dress facedown on a poppy-red cloth. The dancer breathes into the ground as behind her another dancer, costumed the same, runs across the stage and another dancer in the same fawn dress appears bending, touching the ground, raising her own dress up. And then another pliés arms crossed all the way to the ground she touches so tenderly and then two more women run in, meet each other, and walk hand and hand so slowly past the body on the floor facedown on the poppy cloth. They are all dressed the same, are one, but do they even register the body on the ground?

Thirteen female dancers in fawn-colored slip dresses now populate the stage. In her own time each dancer sinks into the earth and spills facedown, and rises up, lifting arms up, and then runs. When the movement is high in the body limbs extend, reaching as if to risk separating from the torso. When the movement is low the body threatens to become part of the earth, collapsing into it. Movement in the midrange is clutching the self to the self rarely tenderly and now with an escalation toward hitting the stomach, clenching into the body. And hands, rubbing, move the dress up and up, hands over ribs, stomach, hips and then across the stage running and leaping in a circular movement reminiscent of ballet although this is not ballet as the other women run-stop-run, join hands and run. This motion brings up the rust-colored peat and sweat, dresses clinging, dirt-smeared, of this they appear unaware. And when did the dancer on the ground get up, now indistinguishable in the crowd? And the poppy cloth left in dirt and the fawn-clad bodies, all only softly differentiated, are the social body moving as one.

A turning of the social body begins, which is inclined toward leaping, as of deer, as of gazelles, as if trying to lift the self from the earth. And one's own hands smoothing over one's own body, washing the body with a liquid of arms and praising the earth, and running to sweep up the poppy cloth. Lift it slowly and slowly move with it, as if it were a revelation while the others around you, exactly like you, move and then seeing the cloth in your hands stop. The cloth now dropped to the ground, now a terror. They gather a flock of tender animals and move, clutch, slide, move, angular, a form of unison-community the cloth an abstracted throb. To feel sex this way, the social body and what is poppy just at the periphery. And so sex is breaking away from this, a danger as the limbs break away from the torso, nature breaking out of the body when movement goes to the upper regions. We hear feet stamp the peat and the social body shudders and throbs toward the poppy cloth, hands drawing the nude dress up.

And upon the entrance of men the women scatter, each dancer now occupying separate space. Thirteen men wearing black trousers, torsos unclothed perform the women's motion but less clenched, and when the men dance we realize the women more capable of whip-like movement, the womanly body here more angular and ribboning as if made to clench, wrap. The red cloth now taken up by one of the women, they pass it off between them, compelled to take it up when it falls, to draw energy which shudders through the body and then, as if compelled, to give it away to another woman, only women, this poppy cloth kept from the men. But this description has too much agency: the women's movements are commanded by the cloth, the men intent on drawing them away from it.

When a woman holds the cloth for long enough she becomes infused with tensile delicacy, movements that register as dance rather than thrust, hit, stomp, kick she cannot stop dancing, cannot be stopped. Is the poppy cloth passion, passion not for men or women but for the body singular moving in space? And when leaping she is caught by a man and the cloth flutters to the ground posing the question of who will take up the cloth now? And now the social body forms a circle patterned boy girl boy girl each body swaying and clenching and slowly walking, the poppy cloth in the middle of the circle flare-red.

With a crescendo the social body falls en masse to the floor, each torso a sharp edge, the circle tightens. How to know who will be chosen to wear the poppy-red cloth? Who will be chosen for the sacrifice? The audience speculates along with the social body on the stage: will this be the one so infused with the dance that when a man intervenes, lifting you, what would otherwise be flight becomes tethered to a tree? Because flight is singular and the men now gathered around encage. Is this the way one becomes a "you," an "I," isolated from who was your body?

The cloth gathered from the dirt as hands slap thighs, this movement suddenly compels the social body, becomes more unified as happens in a time of fear, the original action which had come from the body now becomes a compulsive repetition. Breaking away from the social body a man now lies facedown on the poppy cloth and the women are lifted and fall in rage and they are possessed, the man on the poppy cloth occupying the poppy territory. If one of us does not wear the poppy cloth then we will have given it over to the men, the one facedown on it, claiming it, it is embraced and pinned.

Huddled together we take turns imagining what it would be like to leave the group, to approach the man, to remove him from the cloth by offering ourself to it, become poppy-dressed and so release power from the earth. We know this even while the man's body occupies the sacred space of the fabric. We move in unison again, this time adding water to our gesture of pull and tug, the man now rising from his occupation, we make the same gesture all of us but also separately, something Grecian in our stature always approaching the fabric and backing away until one of us takes it up. She has chosen this and this poppy cloth, this sacrifice, has chosen her like the hand moving toward the flower and the flower moving toward the hand.

She is not yet afflicted although we perhaps are all already afflicted. The chosen one brings the fabric to him as if asking permission to wear it or as if telling him of the fabric's insistency to be held and cradled. He embraces her, and as the others thrust and jump, smear dirt into their bodies, he dresses her in the poppy cloth, the men and women comprising the social body now move in unison but more violent whipping and slapping the ground, and she in red and he standing still while the others dart arrowing into each other with the thrust of sex. And she now walking with him, she has yet to dance wholeheartedly and flung out and the expression of the others is of disdain or hostility, her poppy dress semi-transparent and she walks, pushed by him, clutched by the shoulders, barefoot in the dirt.

What would it mean to occupy her position, to assume her "I"? She is as if beginning to learn how to move although he is still guiding her around by the shoulders, the social body now not hostile moves with little stuttering steps and then not at all. And walking so slowly in her poppy dress she falls to the ground. Breath, a silence, and then leaping up she begins ecstatic dancing, her sacrifice-steps similar to the steps that had been part of the social body but more vigorous, and he is on the ground, lying on his back, arms electrified up as she dances thrusting circular motions consumed with her own movement, angular, and arms whirring overhead then clutched to the waist and when she is not dancing she is staggering and the others only watch, do not try to hold her. She falls to the earth and up again and plunges and rivets and revolves and pulls world into ribs the magnetic attraction now the earth. The body becomes the poppy-red throb, this dance done with eyes closed all contraction and release bringing the air internal until fallen to the ground in a last collapse.

*…Fort! And then a boy on a bike. Da! And then the neighborhood's lost flock of gulls…*

Steeped in so much death, did Freud sigh into the mountain that was his soul when he composed section five of *Beyond the Pleasure Principle*—arriving at the conclusion that pushed past his previous theory of the primacy of the human drive toward pleasure? Did it seem perhaps inevitable to conclude that the first drive, the primary drive, is to return to the nonliving? And what to say, then, of the relationship of the death drive to what Freud saw as the "life-preserving sex drive"—of *Thanatos* to *Eros*? If Eros is biologically and psychologically life-giving, does it not, then, push in the opposite direction to everything else in the self, which flows toward death? Freud puzzles over this eternal struggle, looking to the hyperbolic version of sexuality evident in the sadomasochist and masochist, for in these figures Eros and Thanatos are entwined as one.

Lingering for a moment over the concept of a "primary masochism," Freud mentions in a footnote a "rich and thoughtful article, though one that is unfortunately not fully clear to me" by a Russian physician and one of the first female psychoanalysts, Sabina Spielrein, who, Freud writes, "anticipated a significant part of this speculation." The essay he refers to is a 1912 paper titled "Destruction as the Cause of Coming into Being" in which Spielrein proposes that while Freud may well be correct in thinking that the "I" is based on striving for pleasure and suppressing displeasure, "the personal psyche is governed by unconscious impulses that lie deeper and, in their demands, are unconcerned with our feeling re-actions." These impulses include destruction and a desire for trans-formation, to be moved and shifted by external experience.

Furthermore, in this paper published eight years before *Beyond the Pleasure Principle*, Spielrein—who had been a patient, then a student, and an intimate of Carl Jung's and who would go on to write the first psychoanalytic dissertation by a woman and to be a pioneer of child psychology, and who would be the second woman doctor ever elected to the Vienna Psychoanalytic Society, and who would found a psychoanalytic children's nursery and teach in the university until Stalin bans psychoanalysis in 1936, and who would in her hometown of Rostov-on-Don in Russia be shot along with her daughters by Germans for being Jews in 1942—Spielrein understands in her essay dissolution to be a necessary component of creation. Rather than being pitted in struggle, Spielrein conceives of the sex and death drives as twined conditions necessary for life: "During reproduction, a union of female and male cells occurs. The unity of each cell thus is destroyed and, from the product of this de-struction, new life originates." She notes this destruction in various instances of fertilization and in the moment of sex itself when: "The male component merges with the female component that becomes reorganized and assumes a new form mediated by the unfamiliar intruder. An alteration comes over the whole organism; destruction and reconstruction, which under the usual circumstances always ac-company each other, occur rapidly."

Spielrein's "destruction" and "dissolution" propose a state of transformation, of re-making that might leave the individual *I* behind but is necessary to the process of becoming, which reminds me of the creative state of consciousness, the "over-mind" described by H.D. in her 1919 statement on poetics *Notes on Thought and Vision*: "That over-mind seems a cap, like water, transparent, fluid yet with definite body…into that over-mind, thoughts pass and are visible like fish swimming under clear water.... I visualize it just as well, now, centered in the love-region of the body."

While Spielrein's process is I-annihilating, it differs from Freud's death drive, which is a return to a state of utter nonbeing, as if the self came out of nothingness and must therefore return to nothingness. Furthermore, compare the existential implications of the two views. In *Beyond the Pleasure Principle* Freud gives us an image of the human as a "living vesicle" which "would be killed by the stimuli coming from these [external] energies if it were not provided with a *shield against stimuli*," a shield of consciousness.

Spielrein in contrast to Freud's ego-as-manager presents us with permeability—a self written-through with the external world, a self that reorganizes relationally. She imagines a "female component that becomes reorganized and assumes a new form" in the act of sex and writes that "the depth of our psyche knows no 'I,' but only its summation, the 'We.'" While Freud's ego-consciousness remains fixed, mediating the unconscious, the superego, and the world, in Spielrein's picture the parts revolve: the psyche "considers the ego to be an object observed and subordinated to other objects."

Loss, and transformation. Loss and transformation and loss. Perhaps little Ernst's "o-o-o" was not *Fort* but *OM*, his "da" an *AH*. Sanskrit seed syllables, moons and suns birthed out of the mouth.

# CELESTIAL SPHERE IV

*...a bouquet made of animal skin, flesh, and organs...*

For her project *Not a Rose* (2008-2012) Heide Hatry created 81 still-life sculptures of flowers using hearts, lungs, stomachs, livers, tongues, sex organs, and other parts of animals discarded in the process of human consumption. Posed in natural environments, photographed and given Latinate titles revealing their material, these animal flowers are nearly indistinguishable from the botanical versions they imitate. For example the pink roses of *Spicula linguarum anitum (tips of tongues of ducks)* appear to grow seamlessly from a thorny rosebush.

While the wonderment of a magic trick infuses my initial appreciation of the project, *Not a Rose* resonates more deeply than mere sleight of hand. Hatry's imitations critique contemporary culture's use of the non-human: like the animal meat grown for mass consumption, discarding offal along the way, "the flowers with which we normally surround ourselves are dead sex organs detached from living things, bred explicitly to secure our pleasure, not our sustenance," Hatry writes in her introduction to the project, published as a book of images accompanied by an array of short essays by writers, philosophers, and scientists. Tongues and white hair of deer unfurling as soft pink petals evoke a close connection between beauty and horror, sex and death and "though the images participate in the slaughter," as Lucy Lippard remarks, "they have the decency to be beautiful." Tiny cascading orchids made from the digestive systems of clams entice us to look again at what we take to be beautiful or repulsive, proposing a materiality that resonates in excess of cultural assumptions underlying the ideal.

To look again, a function of art and a necessity. In her 1931 lecture "Professions for Women" Virginia Woolf recounts the two great adventures of her professional life. The first was to kill off the Victorian ideal of the Angel in the House: "She was intensely sympathetic. She was immensely charming. She was utterly unselfish. She excelled in the difficult arts of family life. She sacrificed daily. If there was a chicken, she took the leg; if there was a draught she sat in it…. Above all, she was pure."

This Angel in the House "bothered me and wasted my time and so tormented me that at last I killed her," a necessity not only for obtaining the clarity of mind-space to write, but also for communicating the truth about "human relations, morality, sex"—truth that the charming, cajoling, flattering Angel in the House could never utter. Woolf discusses the Angel in the House as a cultural concept, but her own mother Julia Prinsep Stephen who died when Woolf was only 13 (unsphered, an event described by Woolf as "the greatest disaster") embodied this ideal. Stephen was so self-sacrificing, so engrossed in tending her extended family and doing good works for the sick and poor, that Woolf questions ever having been alone with her for more than a minute.

After her mother's death Woolf would have encountered her mother's likeness publically—not only in surrounding expectations of femininity, but also in the famous photographs taken by Stephen's godmother and aunt, Julia Margaret Cameron. From these images Stephen stares out at us, as she would have stared out at Woolf, with a prophetess's eyes, clear broad forehead, flowing hair. These photographs circulated, Woolf's biographer Hermione Lee notes, inspiring one of Stephen's many admirers, James Russell Lowell, to write to her as "My Pallas Athene," continuing "Age can never disfigure a face like yours." Diamond, utterance, pearl.

Woolf also would have had idealized versions in Edward Burne-Jones's paintings, for which Stephen had served as model. There we find Woolf's mother not as Psyche (although she appears nearly indistinguishable from the figure in *The Wedding of Psyche*), but as Princess Sabra. A pensive English rose dressed as a bride, draped in white linen, laurel crown on her head, Julia-Sabra is on her way to be sacrificed to a dragon. Saint George will ultimately save the Princess, then instruct her to tame the dragon with her belt, and as she leads it into town he will bargain with the terrified citizens: in exchange for their conversion to Christianity he will take the dragon's life.

Lee observes that Woolf uses the word "difficult" whenever she writes about the attempt to translate her mother into writing. *To the Lighthouse*, however, testifies to the success and beauty of the endeavor. It is in action, in gesture, as Lee asserts, that Woolf manages to convey what is otherwise lost, incommunicable. Describing her mother in her 1939 "Sketch of the Past," Woolf recounts Julia as being "very quick; very definite; very upright; and behind the active, the sad, the silent." These features we recognize in Mrs. Ramsay: "She clapped a deer-stalker's hat on her head; she ran across the lawn in galoshes to snatch a child from mischief."

We might also find the three-part structure of the novel, its movement and action, its embodied gestures, to convey something about loss otherwise incommunicable. Constructed, as Woolf was to describe it, like an "H," sections one and three mirror each other as section two, "Time Passes," builds a long corridor between. Through this passageway the novel's house, its objects, and the surrounding natural world come into focus and only in parentheticals do we learn about the lives of the humans who have departed from it. Mrs. Ramsey has died and Mr. Ramsay's arms, "though stretched out, remain empty." The eldest daughter has died in childbirth. "A shell has exploded" in France, the eldest son among the dead. And thus through a window enters the blinding light of world war.

Between the petal of a flower and the tongue of a lamb resides touch and the mouth filling with pearl. Woolf describes in "Professions for Women" the second greatest adventure in her professional life: "telling the truth about my own experiences as a body." How to convey this truth Woolf does not think she has solved, writing further, "I doubt that any woman has solved it yet." Perhaps this truth is unsolvable—the word "rose" will never flower, a headland we wander but cannot pass over. And so instead of solution we come upon discovery: the relationship between subject and object a fire lily made of dried small squids and part of a clam. The self flickering mica in sand.

# SOURCES

Apuleius. *The Golden Ass*. Translated by Sarah Ruden, Yale University Press, 2011.

Bataille, Georges. *Inner Experience*. Translated by Leslie Anne Boldt, State University of New York Press, 1988.

Baum, Kelly. "Shapely Shapelessness: Ana Mendieta's *Untitled (Glass on Body Imprints—Face)*, 1972." *Record of the Princeton University Art Museum*, 2008, vol. 67.

Bausch, Pina. *Frühlingsopfer (Rite of Spring)*. Tanztheater Wuppertal, 1975.

Best, Susan. *Visualizing Feeling: Affect and the Feminine Avant-Garde*. I. B. Tauris, 2011.

Bontecou, Lee, Ann Philbin, and Donna M. De Salvo. *Lee Bontecou: A Retrospective*. Edited by Elizabeth A. T. Smith, Museum of Contemporary Art, 2003.

Bontecou, Lee. *Untitled*, 1961, welded steel, canvas, black fabric, rawhide, copper wire, and soot. 80 1/4 x 89 x 34 3/4 in (203.6 x 226 x 88 cm).

Bryson, Norman. *Looking at the Overlooked: Four Essays on Still Life Painting*. Harvard University Press, 1990.

Burne-Jones, Edward Coley. *The Princess Sabra Led to the Dragon*, 1866, oil on canvas. 42 1/2 x 38 in (108 x 96.6 cm).

— . *The Wedding of Psyche*, 1895, oil on canvas.

Butler, Judith. *Gender Trouble: Feminism and the Subversion of Identity.* Routledge, 1990.

Cheney, Liana De Girolami. "The Oyster in Dutch Genre Paintings: Moral or Erotic Symbolism." *Artibus et Historiae* 8, no. 15, 1987.

Claesz, Pieter. *Still Life with a Skull and a Writing Quill*, 1628, oil on wood, 9 1/2 x 14 1/8 in. (24.1 x 35.9 cm).

Connelly, Joan Breton. *The Parthenon Enigma.* Alfred A. Knopf, 2014.

Doolittle, Hilda. *Notes on Thought and Vision; The Wise Sappho.* City Lights, 1982.

Freud, Sigmund. *Beyond the Pleasure Principle.* Edited by Todd Dufresne, translated by Gregory C. Richter, Broadview Editions, 2011.

Girard, René. *Violence and the Sacred.* Translated by Patrick Gregory, Johns Hopkins University Press, 1977.

Hatry, Heide. *Not a Rose.* Charta, 2012.

Heda, Willem Claesz. *Still Life with Oysters, a Silver Tazza, and Glassware*, 1635, oil on wood, 19 5/8 x 31 3/4 in. (49.8 x 80.6 cm).

Hesiod. *Works and Days; And Theogony.* Translated by Stanley Lombardo, Hackett Pub. Co., 1993.

Judd, Donald. "Lee Bontecou." *Arts Magazine* 39, no. 7, April 1965.

Kusama, Yayoi. *The Infinity Mirrored Room—The Souls of Millions of Light Years Away,* 2013, wood, metal, glass mirrors, plastic, acrylic panel, rubber, LED lighting system, acrylic balls, and water. 113 1/4 x 163 1/2 x 163 1/2 in.

Lee, Hermione. *Virginia Woolf*. A. A. Knopf, 1997.

López, Iraida H. *Impossible Returns: Narratives of the Cuban Diaspora*. University Press of Florida, 2015.

Loy, Mina. *The Lost Lunar Baedeker: Poems of Mina Loy*. Edited by Roger L. Conover, Farrar, Straus & Giroux, 1996.

Mendieta, Ana. "A Selection of Statements and Notes," *Sulfur,* no. 2, 1988.

——. *Corazón de Roca con Sangre* (*Rock Heart with Blood*), 1975, super-8 color, silent film.

——. *Untitled* (*Genesis Buried in Mud*), 1975, super-8 color, silent film.

——. *Untitled* (*Glass on Body Imprints—Face*), 1972, 13 gelatin silver prints, each 10 x 8 in (25.4 x 20.3 cm).

Noland, Carrie. *Agency and Embodiment: Performing Gestures / Producing Culture*. Harvard University Press, 2009.

Speaks, Elyse. "The Terms of Craft and Other Means of Making: Lee Bontecou's Hybrid Trajectory." *Art Journal Open*, April 29, 2013.

Spielrein, Sabina. "Destruction as the Cause of Coming into Being." *Journal of Analytical Psychology*. 39, 1994.

Steichen, Edward. *Isadora Duncan at the Columns of the Parthenon, Athens*, 1921, selenium-toned silver gelatin, 10 × 8 in (25.4 × 20.3 cm).

Taussig, Michael. *Mimesis and Alterity: A Particular History of the Senses*. Routledge, 1993.

Woolf, Virginia. *The Death of the Moth and Other Essays*. Edited by Leonard Woolf, Harcourt, Brace and Co., 1942.

——. *Moments of Being.* Edited by Jeanne Schulkind, Harcourt Brace Jovanovich, 1976.

Zupančič, Alenka. "The Case of the Perforated Sheet." *Sexuation.* Editd by Renata Saleci, Duke University Press, 2000.

# ACKNOWLEDGMENTS

Thank you to Timothy Donnelly and B. K. Fischer at *Boston Review*; Brian Henry and Andrew Zawacki at *Verse*; Jon Thompson at *Free Verse*; Laynie Browne at *Solidarity Texts: Radiant Re-Sisters*; and Rebecca Wolff at *Fence* for publishing pieces from this manuscript, often in different configurations.

Enormous thanks to Susquehanna University for supporting this project. My gratitude to Alan Gilbert, G. C. Waldrep, and Elizabeth Zuba for reading and commenting on drafts of these pieces. To Carla Harryman, my deep appreciation for selecting this manuscript and for the paths of writing, thinking, and being your work has opened. Thank you, Austin Thomas, for lending *Black with Colored Circles* to this sphere. To Andy Fitch, Aimee Harrison, Travis Sharp, Julia Cohen, and Essay Press: thank you for your care with this book and for the innovation you continue to foster.

Author of three books of poetry, *A Conjoined Book* (Omnidawn, 2014), *Iteration Nets* (Ahsahta, 2010), and *Knowledge, Forms, the Aviary* (Ahsahta, 2006), **KARLA KELSEY** has received awards from the Poetry Society of America and the Fulbright Scholars Program. She edits the poetry book review website *The Constant Critic*, and with Aaron McCollough co-publishes *SplitLevel Texts*, a press specializing in hybrid genre projects.

# OTHER TITLES BY ESSAY PRESS

*THE BODY: AN ESSAY* JENNY BOULLY

*LETTERS FROM ABU GHRAIB* JOSHUA CASTEEL

*A PRANK OF GEORGES* THALIA FIELD & ABIGAIL LANG

*GRIFFIN* ALBERT GOLDBARTH

*ADORNO'S NOISE* CARLA HARRYMAN

*I, AFTERLIFE: ESSAY IN MOURNING TIME* KRISTEN PREVALLET

*THE AGE OF VIRTUAL REPRODUCTION* SPRING ULMER

*SINGING IN MAGNETIC HOOFBEAT* WILL ALEXANDER

*THIS IS THE FUGITIVE* MISHA PAM DICK

*IDEAL SUGGESTIONS: ESSAYS IN DIVINATORY POETICS* SELAH SATERSTROM

*LITANY FOR THE LONG MOMENT* MARY-KIM ARNOLD